Sugar Snaps & Strawberries

SUGAR SNAPS & STRAWBERRIES

Simple Solutions for Creating
Your Own Small-Space Edible Garden

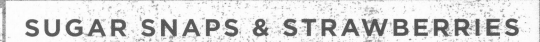

BY Andrea Bellamy
WITH PHOTOGRAPHS BY Jackie Connelly

Timber Press

Portland · London

To my daughter, Lila,
and future gardeners everywhere.

CONTENTS

PREFACE

All around us, a movement is taking place. People are rigging up window boxes for growing herbs, making room on the fire escape for a pot of tomatoes, renovating neglected flowerbeds to make way for raspberries and rhubarb, and convincing landlords to turn over a few square feet of lawn for food production. Families are joining waitlists for community garden plots, signing up for canning workshops, and getting to know their local growers at the farmer's market.

The economy, self-sufficiency, sustainability, taste, health—whatever your reasons, it is always a good time to grow your own organic food. And you can do it, no matter how small your gardening space.

I grow food for all these reasons, but most of all I do it because it feels great. I love working outside and getting my hands dirty. I love connecting with other gardeners and sharing seeds and ideas. And I love harvesting something I have grown and eating it fresh that night for dinner. Yes, it is local food—really local food. But mainly it's just good food.

For me, gardening has been a lifelong obsession and an experiment in trial and error. Lots of error. And, believe it or not, that is something I love about growing food—it keeps me on my toes. Just when I think I've finally mastered this urban farming thing, nature proves me wrong. The key, I think, is to pay attention—to celebrate each perfect potato, learn from mistakes, and, above all, enjoy the process.

This book walks you through the basics—and then some—of planning, creating, and tending an organic food garden in a small space. This is the book I wish I had when I was a new gardener, and I hope it will be a helpful resource and an inspiration to you. Most of all, I hope you get hooked on gardening and growing your own good food.

ACKNOWLEDGMENTS

This book would never have been written without the love and support of my husband, Ben. Thank you for everything, honey.

I am also eternally grateful to my parents, Bill and Sandi Bellamy. In addition to introducing me to the pleasures of gardening and good food, they were instrumental in giving me the time and support I needed to write. Thank you.

I would also like to give a big shout out to HeavyPetal.ca readers for their encouragement and enthusiasm. I love the cross-pollination of ideas we've got going!

Thanks are also due to Caitlin and Owen Black, Carole Christopher, City Farmer—Vancouver Compost Demonstration Garden, Matt Kilburn, Lorey Lasley, Pat Logie, the Society Promoting Environmental Conservation, UBC Farm, and Nancy Zbik for letting us photograph their beautiful gardens. Special thanks to Caitlin Black at Aloe Designs, Bill Chalmers at Western Biologicals, Richard Reynolds of GuerrillaGardening.org, Rin at the Farmhouse Farm, and Maninder Tennessey at Atlas Pots for sharing your time and expertise. Thanks to Leslie Courchesne, Randy Friesen, and Vivian Garfinkel for helping me find the time to write. And thanks to my friends for just being there.

Thanks to Jackie Connelly for the amazing photography.

Thanks to the gang at Timber Press, especially Juree Sondker.

And, finally, I'd like to thank worms for doing so much of the grunt work. You guys rock.

GARDEN STYLE

Not all that long ago, vegetable gardens were relegated to the backyard. Tucked away from the eyes of neighbors and visitors, the veggie patch was often plain and utilitarian. It served one function: to feed the family.

Now, edibles are everywhere—even on the grounds of the White House. And not only gardeners are doing the growing. Foodies are discovering the beauty of cooking with homegrown produce and herbs. Self-sufficient types are learning how to feed themselves—from seed to plate. And we are all trying to lighten our carbon footprint and save money by eating closer to home. Finally, the veggie patch is having its day.

Opposite: There is beauty in a garden, no matter how simple or how small.

Few of us have a spare 200 square feet in which to hide a vegetable garden. In a small space—be it a balcony, a patio, a plot in a community garden, or even a small yard—everything is right there in front of you. So forget about segregating your edibles—celebrate them! Put your veggie patch on display. You're living with it—and, in summer, practically in it—so you may as well design your edible garden to be beautiful as well as functional.

You might be entering the food-growing game for reasons not too different from those of your grandparents. You might just want a basic, yet productive, vegetable patch from which to supplement your meals. But even a no-frills approach to food gardening can be attractive. It starts with a bit of dreaming and planning, which is what this chapter is all about.

FINDING YOUR PERSONAL STYLE

Deciding how you want your garden to look can be a difficult task. You might find yourself drawing a blank—or having many differing visions of your personal paradise.

Take a moment to disregard the reality of your space. Forget its limitations. Let your mind wander and think about your dream garden. What do you imagine? It could be the charming, formal kitchen garden at a bed and breakfast you visited in France. It could be your grandfather's sun-drenched veggie patch behind the old house, or the casual luxury of the penthouse suite deck you can see from your balcony.

Finding and embracing these inspirations will set the theme, or mood, of your garden. And although you might not be able to duplicate your dream garden at home, you can use its characteristics to influence your garden design.

You may not have room for a traditional potager, for example, but you can incorporate touches of this time-honored French kitchen garden design into any space. Choose weathered terracotta or metal planters, planting one with boxwood (*Buxus sempervirens*), the evergreen shrub traditionally used to hedge in a potager, to provide structure and year-round greenery. Your choice of plants (attractive edibles combined with ornamental flowering plants) and structure (formal and geometrical rather than informal and asymmetrical) will all hint at the theme of your garden space.

An obvious theme for your garden isn't necessary, of course. But keeping that one overarching idea—your dream garden—in mind will help you stay on track as you choose containers and make other design decisions.

You can find inspiration in many places.

o **Your home.** The mood of a favorite room can be re-created in your outdoor space.

o **Your travels.** A favorite vacation spot can be your muse.

o **Your neighbors' gardens.** Peek over fences and check out what's growing in your neighbors' backyards to get clues about what plants grow well in your area.

o **Memory.** The gardens of childhood often leave lasting impressions; perhaps you can re-create a favorite in your own space.

o **Local garden centers and botanical gardens.** These organizations often have drool-inducing displays and ideas you can borrow.

Also check out garden books and magazines; garden, home design, and style blogs; and online photo galleries such as Flickr. Inspiration is everywhere.

. . . .

Opposite, top: Red cabbage takes center stage in a mixed ornamental and edible border.

Opposite, bottom left: Potager is a French term for an ornamental vegetable garden. This traditional, intensive design often combines herbs and flowers with attractive vegetables in geometric patterns and beds.

Opposite, bottom right: Accessorizing your outdoor space makes it feel personal and welcoming. Lanterns in an apple tree help set the mood in this garden.

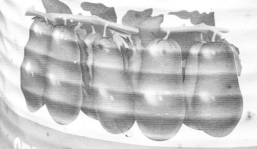

If you like wildly different design styles and can't decide on one, this chapter describes the differences between formal and informal garden styles to help you determine whether you prefer one over the other. This can be a starting point for your design. Or borrow a technique used by interior decorators, fashion designers, and creative types from all fields and create a mood board—a collection of images, objects, text, and textures that provide a visual illustration of your garden ideas. Collect images and objects that inspire you and arrange them on poster board, in a notebook, or online. Start big, choosing a lot of images, and then weed out the pieces that don't fit in. This will help clarify your style preference and provide direction for a clear final vision.

Designing for small spaces

Designing a small garden comes down to a lot of tough choices. Rarely is there room for everything you want to include in your space, so you have to do a bit of soul searching to make decisions about what is really important. Do you want to make a dedicated effort to grow as much of your own produce as possible? Or do you want to grow only a few herbs to support your cooking habit? What else needs to be able to happen in your growing space—besides growing? Would you sacrifice a barbecue for a couple of blueberry bushes? The desired scale of food production will have a huge impact on how your garden will look.

For me, gardening is a balancing act. I aim to grow as much food as I can in my small space, while still allowing room for things other than plants—a barbecue, a place to eat, even a corner where my daughter can splash in a wading pool. Style-wise, I am a contradiction, loving the clean, modern lines of minimalism, yet coveting the sensory overload of an abundant veggie plot. I am lucky because I have both a balcony and a community garden plot, and therein lies my personal solution: keep it neat and restrained at home, and go wild in the allotment.

Opposite: Look for beauty and inspiration in everyday objects. *Below:* Gardeners must balance multiple demands in a small outdoor space. Through careful planning, this gardener produces a lot of food on a modest patio and still has space to relax.

As much as I sometimes covet a big backyard, I know that some blessings come with a small garden. A small garden forces you to be organized, because you have no place to hide junk or plants and containers that you don't really like. (And you'll like your garden more after you have edited it.) The best thing about a small garden is that it is manageable. No need to spend hours fussing over, well, anything—unless you want to. Gardens can take a lot of work, so it can be best to start small no matter how big your garden space. Forget the yard envy, and focus all your efforts on making your little space as beautiful and as productive as possible.

A QUICK GARDEN DESIGN LESSON

In designer-speak, gardens can usually be divided into two types: formal and informal. Of course, some combine the best of both.

Get familiar with a few of the basic principles behind these styles, because this can help you identify common elements in the types of gardens you find appealing. And understanding the key characteristics of gardens you love will help you to create something just as beautiful in your own space.

Formal garden designs

Formal garden designs emphasize order, symmetry, and geometry. But even if you think of yourself as a casual, rule-bending personality type, don't dismiss formality entirely. Vegetable gardens are traditionally laid out with straight rows and rectangular plots for a reason.

Humans are predisposed to finding appeal in the repetitive harmony of a formal design. Pattern is pleasing—whether it is introduced through a series of perfectly aligned raised beds, in fruit trees in identical containers marking the four corners of a patio, or in a variety of red and green lettuces grown in patchwork squares.

Formal designs also tend to work well with urban architecture—from the geometry of a city skyline to the straight lines of your own home.

. . . .

Below: Grains such as wheat and buckwheat add interest and movement in an informal edible garden.

Opposite, top: This garden's design is asymmetrical, yet it feels orderly; some of the best garden designs are successful because they blend formal and informal elements.

Opposite, bottom: Repetition, symmetry, and pattern work to make this patio container garden a modern, comfortable space.

Finally, formal gardens tend to hold their shape—and their interest—year-round. Even when your crops are buried under snow, the rhythm and balance of a formal garden will still be clearly defined by the placement and outline of beds, containers, arbors, and obelisks.

Informal garden designs

If flowing curves, a casual or eclectic look, a "natural" appearance, or an edible landscape appeal to you, you might prefer informal garden designs.

Compared to the obvious symmetry and geometry of formal garden designs, informal gardens can seem haphazard and wild (frankly, sometimes they are). But the best informal designs use some of the same principles used in formal garden designs—balance and pattern—yet use them in a different way.

Designing an informal garden often takes more planning than a formal garden design. For example, using formal principles to design a balcony garden, you could buy identical containers and place them neatly along the base of the balcony railing. Regardless of what you plant in the containers, their placement will have a satisfying rhythm. Put in a little more effort by thinking about creating symmetry through the edibles you choose, and you're golden.

In contrast, if you want to create an informal design on that same patio, you might choose several different, yet harmonious, containers in various colors and materials, and arrange them in eye-pleasing groups of three and five. (Groups of odd numbers of items look more natural than do groups of even-numbered items.) You could then choose and place plants with an eye to creating a balance of colors, textures, and forms.

When created without planning or foresight, an informal garden—whether edible, ornamental, or a mix—can become a messy and visually unappealing mishmash. Of course, sometimes it can look awesome. Some people just have a gift for gardening by the seat of their pants.

. . . .

Opposite: The upright leaf form of alliums such as leeks provide good contrast to lower growing edibles with rounded or oblong leaves.

DESIGNING AN EDIBLE GARDEN

No matter what look you're going for, a few key design principles can help you create a gorgeous edible garden.

- Repetition, contrast, balance, and pattern: keep these concepts in mind when planning your informal garden.

- Aim for a variety of leaf shapes in your planting. Contrast crinkly leafed chard with ferny carrots and large-leafed squashes with the tall, slim straps of leeks.

- Think about plant form—for example, climbing, mounding, or cascading—when planning your planting scheme. Visualize how these shapes will look together.

- Use colorful varieties of edibles: bright, bold rhubarb; scarlet runner beans; dusky purple cabbages; jewel-toned eggplants and peppers.

- Dotting groups of similar plants throughout the garden ties the space together and creates a sense of harmony and balance, and adding plants with contrasting forms, colors, and leaf shapes adds interest.

- Don't take a one-here, one-there approach to planting. In informal gardens, place plants in odd-numbered groups or swaths for best impact.

- Taller plants should be at the back of your bed, unless you intentionally want them to shade shorter plants. That said, some variation is definitely appropriate—take too rigid an approach to height ordering, and your plants will look like they have lined up for a class photo. The word *undulate* is good to keep in mind as you visualize your informal planting scheme.

EDIBLE LANDSCAPES AND FOREST GARDENS

In an edible landscape, some, most, or all the plants are edible. Your design can be as basic as tucking attractive herbs, veggies, and edible flowers into an existing ornamental garden, or as complex as designing a self-sustaining garden that mimics the natural forest ecosystem. In essence, edible landscaping recognizes that food-producing plants and trees can be attractive enough to hold their own in any garden. Why plant something just because it looks pretty when you can plant something that will produce food and also look good?

Think about a typical single-family home on an urban lot with basic landscaping: a tree or two, shrubs around the perimeter of the house, some flowers planted along the front walk. Nothing fancy. But if the space were designed using edible landscaping principles, the trees would be fruit- or nut-bearing, the shrubs would produce berries, and the flowers would be edible. Perhaps grapevines or kiwifruit would clamor up an arbor, with swaths of grains, herbs, sunflowers, and pumpkins edging the house.

An edible forest garden takes the concept of edible landscaping a lot further. A forest garden is designed to replicate a woodland ecosystem, with food-producing trees, shrubs, and plants that work together in layers or stories—just like in a natural forest. Forest gardening comprises seven layers:

- **the overstory** (large fruit and nut trees)
- **the understory** (smaller trees)
- **shrubs** (berry shrubs and cane fruits)
- **herbs** (vegetables and herbs)
- **groundcovers** (low-growing edible plants)
- **roots** (root vegetables and mushrooms)
- **vines** (edible vines)

Each layer in a forest garden supports the other layers, performing multiple functions beyond food production. Trees, for example, hold water in the soil with their extensive root systems, provide support for scrambling vines, and create leaf mulch in the fall. Forest gardens are usually designed to be largely self-supporting, using perennials and self-seeding annuals to avoid the yearly spring plant-a-thon so familiar to most food gardeners.

Although planting a large tree may not be feasible for most small-space gardeners, forest gardens can be created on a smaller scale—even centered around one small tree.

Even the smallest spaces can be beautiful and productive gardens that show amazing style. After all, it's not the size that matters; it's how you use it.

ORNAMENTAL EDIBLES

Many ornamental edibles, such as those listed here, are attractive enough to be the focus of a container or garden bed. Fill out your plantings with tall, airy grains such as amaranth, flax, or quinoa and provide year-round structure with a perennial shrub such as blueberry or any fruit tree. Edible flowers such as borage, calendula, chamomile, lavender, marigold, nasturtium, and sunchoke provide the colorful icing on the cake.

artichoke	fennel	rosemary
basil	grapes	runner beans
beets	kale	sage
cabbage	kiwi	sorrel
chard	leeks	squash
chives	lettuce	strawberries
cilantro	mushrooms	sunflower
dill	parsley	thyme
eggplant	rhubarb	

Opposite: Fruiting shrubs such as blueberries provide low-maintenance structure to an edible landscape or forest garden. Photo by Andrea Bellamy.

Right: Artichokes are large, sculptural plants that provide interest and structure in an edible landscape.

ASSESSING YOUR SPACE

Although we can carefully select our containers and meticulously plan a planting scheme, short of leveling trees or neighboring buildings, we can't do much about the sunlight our gardens receive.

External factors have a huge influence on the success of a garden; take the time to observe these in your space before leaping in and planting. Don't despair if, at first glance, your potential location seems unsuited to growing food. Think creatively: the problem is often the solution. Working with what is already available on your site will always be more satisfying and will yield better results than fighting natural conditions.

Opposite: Before you don your gloves and dig in, take some time to observe what is already happening on your site.

When sizing up your space, considering a few external factors can help you design the healthiest, most productive garden possible.

CLIMATE

Where you live determines your garden's climate, the length of the growing season, and how much rainfall you receive—all of which affect what you grow and how you grow it. Some edibles simply grow better in some regions than they do in others. Recognize the characteristics of your climate, and consider how they will impact what you can grow.

For example, drought-tolerant rosemary, a Mediterranean native, needs dry, hot summers to thrive. That doesn't mean it can't be grown in rainy, mild climates, but you should try to create conditions that resemble rosemary's native habitat: provide excellent drainage by amending the soil with sand or perlite, and plant it in the sunniest spot in the garden.

Your area's hardiness zone is another important consideration. Every city or region is assigned a zone number based on its lowest average annual temperature—from Fairbanks, Alaska (zone 1), to Mazatlan, Mexico (zone 11), and everything in between. Plants are also given a zone rating, which offers gardeners a hint as to whether that type of plant will survive the winter in their area. For example, if you live in Halifax, Nova Scotia, zone 6, you should look for plants that are hardy (frost-tolerant) to zone 6 or lower.

The trouble with zone ratings, however, is that a plant's ability to thrive in a certain location depends on more than just minimum temperatures—rainfall and soil conditions, for example, also play big roles in hardiness. Plants grown in containers are also less cold-tolerant than their in-ground counterparts—something else to consider when choosing what and where to grow. You can find out which zone you live in by searching online for "plant hardiness zones."

All that said, hardiness zones don't even come into play as far as annual edibles are concerned—most of these plants will not survive the winter anyway. But zones are definitely an important factor when you're growing plants such as fruit trees or perennial herbs.

A microclimate is an area in which the climate differs from the larger area around it: hotter, cooler, wetter, or drier, a microclimate can be as small as a balcony or as large as a valley. Many factors can change the microclimates of your garden: light bouncing off a patio or wall, heat radiating from a metal fire escape, a wind tunnel created between buildings, or a clothes dryer that vents onto your balcony. Pay attention to these factors and, if you can, use them to your advantage.

FOR EVERYTHING THERE IS A (GROWING) SEASON

The growing season refers to the length of time between your area's last killing frost in winter or spring and the first killing frost in autumn or winter—basically, it describes the season during which plants grow. Government organizations such as Environment Canada or the National Climatic Center in the United States track these dates and make them available online (search "average frost dates" or "growing season length").

The length of your growing season will help determine what you can plant, since some plants—melons, for example—require a long, hot growing season. Seed packets often provide the number of days required for a seed to grow into a harvestable vegetable (known as days to maturity). If that number exceeds the number of days in your growing season, you should start your seeds indoors ahead of your last frost date and transplant them outside after the weather has warmed, protect the plants from late-season frosts until they can be harvested, or choose a variety that is quicker to mature.

Opposite, top: Herbs such as sage, rosemary, and lavender are happiest if you keep their Mediterranean origins in mind: plant them in a sunny place with well-drained soil.

Opposite, bottom: Concrete walls act as heat sinks, collecting warmth from the sun during the day and releasing it at night. You can take advantage of the microclimate created by these walls by growing heat-loving plants and fruit trees nearby, or by using them to support vines such as kiwi.

LIGHT

Sunlight—or lack of it—is a huge factor in a garden. Most fruits and vegetables require upward of six hours of direct sunlight daily to thrive. A sunny balcony or garden is considered ideal (you can always create shade if you or your plants are baking), but any patio that receives some sunlight in summer can produce food.

Make a point of recording how many hours of direct sunlight your site receives and where it falls. Then work with the amount of light you have. Planting sun-loving vegetables such as tomatoes or cucumbers in shade will just make you, and your plants, unhappy. Instead, plant edibles for part shade, or, if you really are in the dark, grow mushrooms.

If the exterior walls of your home are white, remember that sunlight will bounce off the surface, providing additional light (and heat). You can mimic this effect by setting up a reflective panel such as a mirror or foil-covered board (or mitigate it using a dark color).

SOIL

Your soil has such an impact on the success of your garden that I have devoted a whole chapter to it (chapter six). If you're planning on growing food in the ground (rather than in containers or raised beds), you can assess your existing soil using the techniques discussed in this book.

EDIBLES FOR PART SHADE

An area receiving approximately four hours of sunshine daily is in part shade. The standard advice is that, in these conditions, you can rule out heat-loving fruiting vegetables such as zucchinis, tomatoes, melons, and peppers, while leafy greens and berries will thrive. But in my experience, many edibles that prefer full sun—even fruiting vegetables—will produce in part shade. They just won't produce as much. So if you've got your heart set on tomatoes, give them a shot. Seeds are cheap and experimenting is half the fun, anyway. Try these edibles in part shade.

alpine strawberries	currants	peas
arugula	gooseberries	radishes
beets	kale	rutabagas
blackberries	lettuce	scallions
blueberries	mint	sorrel
chard	mushrooms	spinach
Chinese cabbage	mustard greens	
chives	parsley	

Opposite: Peas and beets are good choices for a less-than-sunny locale.

Right: Fruiting vegetables such as cucumbers, tomatoes, peppers, eggplants, pumpkins, and squash need eight or more hours of direct sunlight to be truly productive.

WATER

Along with soil and sun, water makes your garden grow. Or not. Because poor drainage is death to plants, you need to identify whether your site might have pockets where water will pool. (Cold air will also hang out in low-lying areas, creating frost-prone microclimates.)

Your garden should be within easy reach of a hose or tap. Balconies are often lacking in water access, and lugging a watering can from your kitchen sink every day can be a royal pain. Consider installing a rain barrel that catches and stores rainfall to reduce your trips to the tap (and the impact on storm sewers).

WIND

Wind can be a big factor in the city, especially on rooftops and balconies. Heavy winds speed moisture loss from the soil, knock over containers, and shred delicate leaves. Mulching reduces soil moisture loss, and windbreaks provide shelter for tender vegetables. A fence or trellis covered in an edible climber such as runner beans or blackberries makes a great windbreak. Grouping containers together will help keep them from toppling over.

SIZE

Small-space gardening means different things to different people: it could mean a 4 ft. by 8 ft. (1.2 by 2.5 m) raised bed in a community garden, or a tiny window box. Obviously, the size of your site impacts what you can grow; some edibles just aren't practical in a tiny garden. Of course, you can always look for more space.

WEIGHT

If you garden on a balcony or rooftop, weight is an important consideration. Containers, soil, plants, water, and people add up to a heavy load. Consult with your landlord or an engineer or builder on weight restrictions to ensure that your balcony is up to the task.

You can reduce the load by choosing lightweight containers such as plastic, resin, or fiberglass; using the light and airy soil specifically designed for container growing; and taking the weight off the floor with wall- and railing-hanging planters and hanging baskets.

Left: Container size limits plant size and options—but not visual impact.

Opposite: Hanging baskets are a great way to gain extra gardening space—and they keep the weight load down on your balcony.

POLLUTION

You are growing food to eat, and you want healthy, organic edibles. But if your efforts are undermined by pollution, you may be inadvertently consuming contaminants. Fortunately, you can usually lessen pollution's effect on your plants by making sure your soil is healthy and free of toxins.

Before you begin working in existing soil, check to determine what was on your land before you were. Could it have been a gas station? A tannery? A dry cleaners? Chemical contaminants from industrial businesses can devastate the soil for generations.

If you are in doubt about this aspect of your soil, build raised beds using new soil, or, if you're set on gardening in the ground, get your soil tested before you plant.

Do not grow edibles near patios or beds built using treated lumber: its chemical preservatives leach into surrounding soil. You should also avoid growing food next to busy streets; along with the vehicles' exhaust, cars tend to cloak plants with a film of grit. If the only space you've got is street-side, grow root vegetables to avoid most of the grime.

PESTS

At some point as a gardener, you will curse a pest for a) peeing in your garden, b) digging up your seedlings, or c) wolfing down your almost-ready-to-pick produce. This is pretty much a fact. So when designing your garden, you would be smart to look at your space with an eye for potential bandits.

Although it is difficult to predict which types of insect pests your garden will attract, unless you're gardening on a high-rise balcony, urban gardeners can count on visits from raccoons, squirrels, rats, cats, and dogs. In suburban and rural areas, deer, rabbits, and groundhogs join the fun. Finally, consider the human pest. Native to both country and city, some humans miss the value in a garden. If your garden is exposed to the public, you can probably expect litter, crushed or broken plants, and theft.

If deer or dogs might be an issue, consider a fence to keep deer at bay and prevent dogs from trampling and peeing on your garden. Line the bottom of raised beds with hardware cloth to deter burrowing animals such as moles and groundhogs if they're an issue in your area. In high-traffic locations, a low fence can help define your space and prevent people from stepping on your plants.

PROXIMITY

You may not have much of a choice where your garden is located, but situating it as close as possible to where you conduct your daily activities, especially cooking, is always a good idea. Consider how you move through and interact with your space, and lay out your garden appropriately. For example, if you walk down your front steps and across your front lawn to the sidewalk every day, perhaps the best place for your crops is along this route. You will be more aware of how your garden is faring and more likely to tend to it if you see it several times daily.

Left: If your soil has a sordid past, build up. Raised beds keep your crops off the ground.

Opposite: Dissuade larger pests such as cats from digging in newly cultivated beds by covering them with chicken wire or by keeping exposed soil frequently watered—they seem to prefer digging in dry beds.

COMMON SITE PROBLEMS

PROBLEM	WORKING AROUND IT	WORKING WITH IT
Too much heat	Erect screens or trellises to provide shade.	Grow drought-tolerant, heat-loving plants; grow a screen of heat-lovers to create shade for more sensitive plants.
Not enough sun	Reflect light using mirrors; reduce shade by removing branches or trees if applicable.	Grow shade-tolerant plants and fungi.
Short growing season	Start seedlings indoors weeks before the last frost date; provide protection from late-season frosts.	Grow edibles that can be planted and harvested within a short window of time; grow hardy perennials.
Poor soil	Remove old soil and replace it with new soil; build raised beds.	Grow edibles that are tolerant of poor soils while working to remediate it over time by amending with organic matter and growing soil-improving plants.
Inconvenient water access	Lug watering cans from the nearest tap; invest in drip irrigation or rain barrels.	Grow drought-tolerant plants.
Poor drainage	Grow in raised beds or containers.	Amend soil with sand and organic matter; grow plants that like damp soil.
Heavy winds	Erect fences or trellises; group containers to provide stability.	Plant a screen of wind-tolerant plants to shelter tender edibles.
Little growing space	Find garden space elsewhere.	Grow vertically; practice succession planting and other small-space techniques.

CONTAINER GROWING VERSUS IN-GROUND GARDENING

For many (balcony and rooftop gardeners in particular), growing in the ground is not an option. But if you do have a choice, you might assume that growing plants in the earth is inherently better than growing them in containers. Containers do, however, offer several advantages.

○ **You can have perfect soil.** Plants perform best if you cater to their soil preferences, and containers make it easy to give them what they want. For example, carrots are notorious for needing their soil just *so*. Your garden soil might be heavy clay—torture to a carrot—but you can use the lightest, fluffiest sandy loam in at least one container for carrots.

○ **You can move them around.** Cool-season crops such as beets and spinach may enjoy full sun in early spring, but come midsummer, they will quickly bolt if forced to stand in the heat all day. With containers, you can move heat-sensitive plants out of the sun, extending their season (and making room for heat-lovers such as tomatoes).

○ **You can build a garden anywhere.** Sometimes the only gardening space you have available is on your front steps or on the edge of a driveway. Containers don't mind.

○ **Compaction is reduced.** With traditional in-ground gardening, it can be difficult to avoid stepping into your garden bed to sow, weed, and harvest. This leads to soil compaction, which reduces your soil's ability to absorb water and impacts plants' root growth.

○ **Pests and weeds are easier to control.** It should be easier for you to keep on top of weeding and pest control when dealing with a potted garden, because your total garden space is relatively small. And because containers are raised, they are easier to reach when you do need to intervene.

Of course, containers are not all perfection and can have a few major drawbacks.

○ **Containers dry out relatively quickly.** You'll have to water containers more frequently than you would an in-ground garden.

○ **Conversely,** if your container does not have proper drainage, your plants will drown.

○ **Nutrients must be replaced frequently.** The whole frequent watering thing, combined with the fact that container soil is designed to have only modest amounts of organic matter, means that the soil loses its nutrients quickly. You will need to fertilize diligently and replace organic matter (through compost and mulching) regularly.

○ **You can grow almost anything**—even small trees—in a container, as long as the container is big enough. But large containers are often not an option in a small space: they can be too heavy for some balconies, too unwieldy to move into place, or simply too big for the space.

○ **If not properly cared for,** container plants can be prone to attacks by insect pests. Since pests go after weak or stressed-out plants, make sure your plants are happy—well watered, well fed, in appropriately sized containers, and getting enough sun.

You can garden just about anywhere, as long as you choose plants that are suited to the conditions of your site. And although you probably can't change the amount of sunlight your plants receive, or the fact that your rooftop space is prone to high-speed winds, you can often make little adjustments that will make big differences. You may discover that you have a lot more gardening space than you first thought.

. . . .

Opposite: No yard? No problem. Containers offer an almost instant garden space.

FINDING SPACE

Not many people are blessed with a big, open backyard. But even if you don't have a tiny balcony to call your own, you don't have to be content with store-bought veggies. Be creative in finding growing space to expand your empire.

Opposite top: Smart gardeners increased their available space by co-opting a bit of the alley outside their home. This narrow bed is home to espaliered fruit trees, garlic, corn, potatoes, rhubarb, and a worm bin.

Opposite bottom: Community gardens are often colorful, diverse, and welcoming.

COMMUNITY GARDENS

The classic solution to the space-shortage problem, community gardens have been around in various forms for centuries. Whether gardened communally or clearly divided into individual plots, community gardens—and their British counterpart, the allotment garden—can be a great place to get growing. In addition to paying a plot fee, gardeners are usually expected to help out with basic garden maintenance, fundraising, or other tasks.

  o **Pros:** Meet your neighbors, learn from more experienced gardeners, and share resources. Usually, the cost for an allotment or plot is reasonably affordable.

  o **Cons:** You may have to wait a while to get a space; waiting lists can be long. If the garden is far from your home, it can be inconvenient to maintain and harvest. Theft can also be an issue.

SHARED BACKYARDS

Cities are full of underutilized space, much of which is on private residential property. You may have walked by lawn after empty slate of lawn and imagined what you could grow if some of it were yours.

If you have no garden space of your own, consider a shared yard. Nearby friends or relatives might be willing to let you garden on a corner of their property. Another alternative, Sharing Backyards (http://sharingbackyards.com), matches people looking for garden space with those willing to share. You can also try posting a note on a community forum or other online forum, or do it the old-fashioned way and post a note on a bulletin board at your local coffee shop or community center, or even knock on doors of neighbors who might have space to spare. It's all about connecting with your community.

Some people may want to charge you a small fee for the use of their space, while many are just happy to have their yard beautified for little effort on their part. Most property owners would be grateful for a share of the produce. Key to this arrangement is making sure that you keep your plot looking tidy and that you are respectful of the property owner's tools, utilities, and space.

  o **Pros:** Meet your neighbors, make a friend or two, and gain access to garden space.

  o **Cons:** Can take a lot of legwork to find the right space and property owner to share with. Can be unstable—the property could be sold or leased to new renters who are not into sharing, or the property owner could decide that the situation isn't working, halfway through your growing season.

GARDENING AT WORK

Forward-thinking employers are keen to offer wellness benefits to employees. A workplace garden supports a healthy lifestyle and provides opportunities for workers to be physically active, connect with coworkers, and relieve stress—all things that are valuable to employers. Plus, workplace gardens make the company look good from a sustainability and community engagement perspective—a key selling feature if you decide to approach your boss about a garden project.

Before you ask your employer about creating a garden, think about whether you want to take over an existing garden space for your personal use or create a multiple-user garden—a community garden for the workplace. You should also determine how and where the garden will be constructed, who will maintain it, and on whose time this maintenance will occur.

. . . .

Opposite, top: A classic community garden approach involves dividing land into small plots gardened by individuals or families. Photo by Andrea Bellamy.

Opposite, bottom: Community gardens often acquire tools for communal use.

- **Pros:** Have fun at work, use your lunch break to de-stress, and garden where you spend a good chunk of your week. Your company might even agree to pay for construction materials.

- **Cons:** Getting the go-ahead could take ages in large or bureaucratic organizations. The soil may be of questionable quality—potentially compacted and polluted with industrial wastes. Coworkers may lose enthusiasm after their initial interest, leaving you to maintain the garden on your own.

GARDENING AT SCHOOL

School gardens have a long history. They have been used to teach children about healthy lifestyles, environmental stewardship, and nutrition, and they help students connect with and build community.

- **Pros:** Connect with and learn from other students or parents, and improve the biodiversity and sustainability of your campus or schoolyard.

- **Cons:** The approval process can be painfully slow. You will probably have to raise funds or get materials donated to build the garden.

Gardening for parents

Many elementary school garden programs involve parents. This is a great way to get into gardening and learn with your child. If your child's school does not have an existing garden, approach the principal and volunteer to lead the project.

Gardening for high school and college students

A rising number of high schools and universities have areas dedicated to community garden–style growing. If your school lacks a garden, approach your student council or ask your favorite teacher to work with you to get one approved and built.

In college, your student association is a good place to start, as are faculty members who teach environmental and social sciences.

. . . .

Opposite: Herbs and flowers grow in a checkerboard pattern at an elementary school.

Below: Squash takes over an unused section of train track on land owned by the railroad but tended by locals. Photo by Andrea Bellamy.

GUERRILLA GARDENING

Empty lots, underused public lands, neglected corporate property—there are endless places to build a garden. Guerrilla gardening is less about creating a garden for yourself than it is about greening the urban environment and reclaiming neglected space for the community. The term *guerrilla* implies sabotage and secretive missions in the dark of night, but you probably won't have to worry about landing in jail if you get caught. Most cities and police forces are tolerant of this sort of vegetative deviance.

Forgotten spaces are everywhere—the wells around street trees, the medians between sidewalks and streets, neglected planter boxes belonging to businesses or the city, strips of dirt edging buildings and alleys—and they're dying for a little bit of love. Look for something near your home, because you will be tending it on an almost daily basis if you choose to grow time-intensive annual vegetables. Choose a spot close to an available water tap; otherwise, you will be lugging jugs of water to the site. Finally, be aware that guerrilla gardens are impermanent. You should be prepared to find them mowed down by the city landscaping crew or bulldozed once the empty lot you've been tending finally gets developed.

○ **Pros:** Meet curious passersby, feed your community, and beautify neglected spaces. Possibly even harvest a meal or three!

○ **Cons:** Lack of water access, poor soil quality, and possible harassment from authorities or landowners. Property owners may decide to reclaim their land—or simply boot you off—at any time.

THE GUERRILLA'S GARDEN

By Richard Reynolds, author of *On Guerrilla Gardening* and founder of GuerrillaGardening.org

There is something particularly delicious about a crop you have grown on land someone else abandoned; it's a transformation of human trash into nature's treasure. But doing it without the negligent landowner wanting the fruits of your labor or a stake in the ground requires a bit of guerrilla gardening—in other words, doing it without asking first.

Guerrilla growing edibles serves one of two purposes, and you are best choosing which from the start. The first objective is to provide a feast for your stomach. Question if the land is polluted—there are soil testing kits and bioremediation techniques to investigate (for example, sunflowers help remove lead and oyster mushrooms can break down oil)—and use fresh soil and containers if necessary. You may also need to devise a way of disguising your harvest from snackers, mixing edibles among ornamentals or choosing locations away from loitering pedestrians.

Alternatively, growing guerrilla edibles can be done as a feast for the mind—to surprise people by showing them the potential in an overlooked space. Make an optimistic step towards reclaiming the space legitimately by creating a thought-provoking edible public landscape. In these circumstances you want to make sure the crop is seen, so choose familiar plants (such as corn, tomatoes, and strawberries) and plant visibly. The harvest can be shared with bugs, bees, and any grazing passerby.

Opposite: Some community gardens dedicate areas to plants that attract beneficial insects. This buckwheat patch attracts bees from nearby hives.

BOMBING WITH SEEDS

Seed bombs, also known as seed balls, are effective tools for distributing seeds. Each ball contains the basic essentials to get seeds off to a good start. They are often used by guerrilla gardeners in reclaiming derelict and barren sites because they can colonize large areas with only a little grunt work. Simply toss the balls onto a site (do not plant them) and wait for rain, which will kick-start the seeds' growth. The clay and compost protects seeds from being eaten by birds or scattered by wind until they have a chance to germinate.

This is a fun project to do with friends. Using a 16-ounce (474 ml) cup as a measure for each part in the recipe will yield approximately 300 seed bombs. That's a lot of bombing action! After they dry, go out and do some "illicit gardening." It's good, not-so-clean fun.

Ingredients

- 5 parts dry red or brown clay*
- 3 parts dry organic compost
- 1 part seeds**
- 1 to 2 parts water

Steps

1. Thoroughly mix together the dry clay, compost, and seeds.
2. Slowly add water until the mixture holds together without crumbling; it should not be too wet.
3. Pinch off small chunks of the mixture, rolling each chunk into a ball of approximately 2 in. (5 cm) in diameter.
4. Set the balls on cardboard trays or cookie sheets until they are completely dry (two to three days).
5. Scatter them wherever you want new plants to grow.

Ingredient notes

*   Dry red or brown clay is the stuff that potters use. You want the dry powder so it can be easily mixed (it commonly comes premoistened, which is not what you want). Ask for it at an art supply store, or check with a potter's guild to find out where you might obtain some.

**   In choosing seeds, avoid species that are potentially invasive, such as mint. For reclaiming neglected spaces and increasing biodiversity, choose self-seeding herbs, grains, and vegetables such as arugula, mache (corn salad or lamb's lettuce), dill, flax, kale, parsley, and mustard. Attract beneficial insects with anise hyssop, fennel, and calendula. Crimson clover makes an excellent base for your seed mixture because the seeds can be bought cheaply in bulk. Although not edible, crimson clover is an attractive, beneficial insect-attracting crop that adds valuable organic matter and nutrients to the soil.

A GARDEN ANYWHERE

Even if you don't have a balcony or backyard, you probably have more space than you realize. It just takes a little creative thinking to see it. I didn't have the space to grow both peas and beans inside the confines of my patio, for example, so I co-opted the back side of my fence, which separates my patio from an alley. In only a narrow strip of soil at the base of the fence, I planted a family of pole beans, which climb up twine attached to the fence.

Take a look at your back alley: could you install narrow raised beds along the alley's edge? Take a look at your sidewalk: could you grow food in the space between it and the street? Take a look at any hard outdoor surfaces: could you have a container garden on your driveway, porch, fire escape, or staircase? Take a look at your rooftop: is it flat and relatively easy to access? (Remember that you will have to get pots, soil, and water up there, too.) Could it support the weight of a container garden? Take a look at the land surrounding your building: could you convince your landlord, condominium association, or strata council to let you start a garden?

Take a critical look at your space; you may be surprised to find that you have more room than you thought.

Opposite: The gardeners behind this canoe planter must meet a lot of their neighbors; the old canoe, planted with beans, lettuce, peppers, herbs, and chard, is parked just off the sidewalk.

Right: 'Fortex' pole beans grow up a sunny exterior panel of my fence. Photo by Andrea Bellamy.

BUILDING YOUR GARDEN

After you have chosen a site and a garden style, you can start thinking about how you want to build your garden. Perhaps you have already decided how it will grow—you want an informal container garden or a traditional in-ground plot, for example—based on your reflections so far. Or perhaps you are not sure what you need. In either case, read on. This chapter details the best methods of creating growing space, from no-till sheet mulching, to building raised beds and choosing containers.

Opposite: Unless you have inherited a ready-to-plant bed or garden, you must create your own. Chalk up another plus for community gardens—often, the construction is complete or is accomplished as a team.

GARDENING ON BALCONIES, PATIOS, AND OTHER HARD SURFACES

When gardening on a rooftop, balcony, or other similar place lacking in soil, your only option is to bring in containers. Luckily, you can find a nearly endless variety of container styles—from rustic, to modern and everything in between. And you can grow almost anything in a container, even fruit trees, if the container you choose is large enough to accommodate it.

When you are choosing containers, keep a few considerations in mind.

- **Containers are water hogs.** The smaller they are, the more often they need water. Buy a size or two bigger than you need, and you will be grateful come the summer heat wave. Or look for self-watering containers; they can be expensive, but will greatly reduce your number of trips to the tap. Mulching will help reduce evaporation—and refills of the watering can.

- **Bad drainage rots roots.** If your container does not drain properly, your plants will suffer. Skip the saucers, because they trap water. Use container "feet" that raise your pots an inch or so off the ground if you are concerned about stains on your patio. And always use a container with a drainage hole.

- **Container size limits plant size.** If you have your heart set on growing a large plant such as a shrub or tree, be kind and give it the room it needs to thrive.

- **Not all containers are created equal.** That cute little pot might look like a bargain, but will it survive the winter? Unless you live in an area that never requires you to put away your flip-flops, you should make sure that the containers you choose can withstand cold winter temperatures—or be prepared to bring them inside to live with you all winter. Similarly, resin, fiberglass, and plastic containers are available in a range of qualities, from cheaply made to commercial grade. If you want a pot that will last more than one season, invest in high quality containers.

Above: 'Ichiban' eggplants, chives, Cuban oregano, and 'Red Russian' kale thrive in containers on a sunny patio.

Opposite: Planter feet can be simple and inconspicuous or ornate and decorative.

PREPARING A CONTAINER FOR PLANTING

○ **Step one: clean.** When planting in used or recycled containers, you should clean and sterilize them before adding the soil and seed or plant. Mold, disease, and fungi can lurk in used containers, which can then infect your healthy new plants. Sterilization is critical for pots in which you intend to start seeds, because seedlings are susceptible to a fungal disease known as damping-off, which can be transferred through contaminated pots.

To clean a pot, first remove any dirt or plant debris. Rinse the container, and then soak it overnight in a solution of water and hydrogen peroxide or bleach. (About one part hydrogen peroxide or bleach to nine parts water ought to do the trick.) Scrub the pot with a stiff brush if necessary, rinsing thoroughly to remove any traces of cleaning agents, and then set it aside to dry.

○ **Step two: provide drainage.** Providing good drainage is important to healthy container crops. Unfortunately, the containers we fall in love with don't always come with drainage holes. Rather than pass them by—or use them sans drainage hole—you can drill a hole yourself. (Good shops will offer to do this for you.) This is pretty simple to do once you get your hands on the appropriate tools.

Turn the container upside down. Using a high-speed electric drill fitted with a 1/2 to 5/8 in. (12 to 16 mm) drill bit, drill a hole in the center of each small container, or drill three or more holes in each large container. Press gently as you drill; too much force could crack the container. Choose a masonry or ceramic drill bit for terracotta or ceramic pots; plastic and metal containers can be tackled with a standard bit.

Many gardening books and magazines recommend adding a layer of so-called drainage material to the bottom of containers before planting. Shards of broken pots, sand, gravel, and even foam packing peanuts have been cited as good materials for promoting drainage in containers. Recently, however, this practice has been slammed, with some arguing that it actually inhibits water movement. The jury is still out on this one, but I favor skipping the added layer and focusing on providing soil that promotes good drainage.

Finally—and this is optional—place a coffee filter or piece of screen over the drainage hole to prevent soil loss.

○ **Step three: position your container.** Trust me; you do not want to lift the pot once it is full of soil. Place it as near to its final position as possible.

○ **Step four: choose the best soil and add it to the container.** Look for a premium organic potting soil or container mix (or make your own). Specially blended potting mixtures are lighter than standard garden soil and are designed to promote good air circulation and drainage.

○ **Step five: plant.** Plant some seeds or seedlings.

○ **Step six: water and mulch.** Water in your newly planted seeds or plants. This will help settle the soil, which can sometimes take weeks to compress fully. Keep extra potting soil on hand to top off your containers. I like to top off my containers with an inch or two (2.5 to 5 cm) of rich, black, top-quality bagged soil (minus the perlite, which speckles the soil with white particles) or finished (completely broken down) compost. Not only does this provide nutrients and conserve moisture, but it also makes plants pop.

Types of containers

Almost anything that can hold soil can be a home to a plant. Think beyond the garden center when looking for containers—you may find some brilliant planters that complement your style. An old metal wash bucket can go nicely with a cottage garden theme, or a lime green, straight-sided trashcan will punch up a '60s mod-style patio.

○ **Fiberglass.** Fiberglass is a relative newcomer to the container game. Lightweight and fairly durable, fiberglass planters are usually designed to mimic stone, terracotta, or other types of containers—not always well. When done right, however, fiberglass can be a decent and affordable option. As with all planters, quality matters: cheap fiberglass can buckle, lose its shape, or actually melt.

○ **Glazed ceramic.** A huge range of color and style options are available in glazed ceramics. Designs range from simple to intricate, and colors tend to be deeply hued, lending richness to the garden. What's not to love? Their weight, for one thing. Filled with soil, ceramic pots (and terracotta, for that matter) can be quite heavy. Depending on the temperature at which it was fired, a ceramic container may or may not survive a cold winter freeze; ask before you buy. That said, Vietnamese-made ceramics can usually handle extremely cold weather.

○ **Metal.** From chic stainless steel to lightweight zinc, metal planters come in a wide variety of materials and styles. Although they usually look fabulous and last for years, metal containers absorb heat, causing soil to dry out quickly and potentially burning plants' roots. Because of this, metal planters are unsuitable as a container choice for sunny spots—unless they can be modified. Place a thick layer of insulating material, such as bubble wrap, sheets of cardboard, or something similar, between the container and soil to keep the soil from getting too hot and damaging sensitive roots. Alternatively, nest a slightly smaller plastic pot inside the metal container. Zinc containers, often the cheapest of the bunch, will rust over time and should be treated with rust paint if you want them to last. Because they are so lightweight they can buckle or tip easily.

○ **Plastic and resin.** Although plastic has become unfashionable these days, it does have its uses in the garden. Plastic is the cheapest, most lightweight container material, which is definitely a selling feature, especially for balcony gardens with weight restrictions. Resin and polyethylene are often used to make some decent-looking (if pricey) containers, which are said to resist fading resulting from sun exposure, unlike most plastics. Plastic, polyethylene, and resin all stand up to cold weather.

○ **Terracotta.** These classic clay pots are popular for a reason: they are inexpensive, good-looking, and widely available. Terracotta wicks water away from the soil, which is great for Mediterranean herbs and other plants that tolerate dry conditions. It's not so great, however, for plants that like evenly moist soil, and a hot deck or sunny position can exacerbate this drying effect—you sign up for double water duty if you choose this route. One last thing about terracotta: because of its porosity, it absorbs water, which can cause it to crack in below-freezing temperatures. These pots should not remain outside year-round in areas with cold winters.

○ **Wood.** Infinitely customizable, wood can be styled to suit any garden. Although mass-produced wooden planter boxes all tend to have a similar look, wood can swing many ways. Use rough, reclaimed timbers for affordable, sustainable, rustic style, or use smooth-sanded and oiled slats for a container worthy of any craftsperson.

When building your own planter box, choose a naturally rot-resistant wood such as cedar. Applying tung or linseed oil will help protect wood from moisture. Or you can coat the wood with an eco-stain for longer lasting effects. Never use treated wood; it contains toxic chemicals that can leach into soil.

Opposite: With their vivid hues, glazed ceramic containers become focal points in the garden.

GARDENING IN RAISED BEDS

A raised bed, which is simply an elevated gardening bed, can be built using wood, stone, or concrete frames. Technically, an outer frame isn't necessary in a raised bed, but frames do help define the space and prevent soil from washing away.

Why go to the trouble of building a raised bed if you can simply garden in the ground? Raised beds have a number of advantages over old-school in-ground gardening.

If your native soil is polluted, compacted, or otherwise problematic, you can build a raised bed and bring in fertile soil customized for your specific needs. You can even build a raised bed in areas with no soil, such as on top of driveways and patios. (It is best to stick with regular containers for rooftops, decks, and other areas where direct soil contact might cause drainage or rot issues.)

In addition, the soil in raised beds warms up quicker in the spring, allowing you to get an early jump on the planting season. Since you do not walk in raised beds, you don't compact the soil and thus reduce its ability to absorb water and support the development of roots. Raised beds also mean good drainage, assuming you use the appropriate soil— good news for those with boggy native conditions.

Finally, because they are elevated, raised beds are great for gardeners with mobility and back issues. They can even be designed so that you can access them while seated.

· ·

Opposite: A simple raised bed can be built with scrap wood.

Building a raised bed

A raised bed can be fairly simple to make. Our bed is 3 by 6 ft. (90 by 180 cm) and 1 ft. (30 cm) deep, but if these dimensions don't meet your needs, they can be easily adjusted.

Most raised beds are a maximum of 4 ft. (1.2 m) wide to allow gardeners to reach into the center easily. A good minimum depth for leafy veggies and herbs is 6 in. (15 cm), but if you plan to grow root vegetables, build your bed at least 12 in. (30 cm) deep. If you want to build a frame of only 6 in. (15 cm) in height, and the underlying soil is decent, you can till or loosen the soil and gain a few additional inches of depth.

Options include oiling or eco-staining the wood to extend its life, lining the bottom of the bed

with mesh hardware cloth to keep out burrowing animals such as moles and gophers, fitting copper strips inside the top edge of the bed to deter slugs, and installing PVC hoops to support row covers. You can add one, two, or all four of these options depending on your enthusiasm and situation.

. . . .

Top left: Finished beds are ready to be filled with soil. Photo by Ben Garfinkel.

Top right: Attach two, 3 ft.-long, 2-by-6 boards to the 4-by-4 corner posts. Photo by Andrea Bellamy.

Bottom left: Assemble the frame by attaching the longer 2-by-6s to the short ends. Photo by Andrea Bellamy.

Bottom right: You can attach the PVC pipes, two for each long side, with metal strapping or brackets. Photo by Andrea Bellamy.

HOW TO BUILD A RAISED BED

Shopping list

Untreated cedar wood is recommended.

- Four 6 ft. (1.8 m) 2-by-6 (38-by-140 mm) boards
- Four 3 ft. (1 m) 2-by-6 (38-by-140 mm) boards
- One 4 ft. (1.2 m) 4-by-4 (89-by-89 mm) board, cut into four, 11 in. (28 cm) lengths
- Thirty-two 3½ in. (88.9 mm) #14 (6.15 mm) wood screws (deck screws are ideal)

Optional

- Linseed oil, tung oil, or eco-stain
- Hardware cloth, 3 by 6 ft. (1 by 1.8 m), cut to fit the bottom of the bed
- One 18 ft. (5.5 m) length of copper stripping
- One 10 ft. (3 m) length of 1 in. (25 mm) diameter PVC pipe, cut to four 11 in. (28 cm) lengths
- Two 9 ft. (2.7 m) ½ in. (12.5 mm) diameter PVC pipes
- Eight 1 in. (25 mm) galvanized semicircular brackets, or metal strapping to fit
- Sixteen ½ in. (12.7 mm) #8 (4.17 mm) wood screws

Steps

1. If you plan to oil or stain the boards, do this first, and allow a day or two for them to dry.
2. On a concrete patio or another level surface, set out two, 11 in.-long 4-by-4s and lay one of the 3 ft.-long 2-by-6s on top, with the two 4-by-4 posts flush at each end.
3. Attach the board with a couple of 3½ in. screws.
4. Repeat with the second short board. Make two like this; these will be the short ends of the bed.
5. Stand these sides on edge and position the 6 ft.-long 2-by-6s.
6. Attach these longer boards, one side at a time, with screws, and you've got yourself a raised bed.
7. Move it into place, leveling the surface if necessary.

Now you can attach the copper strips along the inside top edge of the bed to deter slugs from crawling in, line the bottom with hardware cloth if desired, or attach the PVC piping that will support row covers or shade cloth.

To make row cover supports, attach two, 11 in.-long (28 cm) pieces of the 1 in. diameter PVC pipe to the inside of each long side of the bed. Space the pipes 1 to 2 ft. (30 to 60 cm) from each end, and secure them with ½ in. screws and semicircular brackets. These tubes will serve as the holders for the ends of the hoops you will insert if row covers are needed. To make hoops, bend the thinner, ½ in. diameter PVC pipes into semicircles, inserting the ends into the larger, permanent pipes (you could also use flexible young branches for this purpose).

Fill the bed with quality organic soil. For a less expensive option, use the sheet mulching method.

Raised beds are not for everyone and every garden style. They would not suit a naturalistic edible landscape, for example, or you may have existing in-ground beds you want to revitalize. Getting the materials to build the frame can be challenging if cost or transportation is an issue. And for gardeners with access to great soil, in-ground gardening is a quick and inexpensive way to get started.

If gardening in the ground sounds like your thing, you have a couple of options for preparing the soil, and they boil down to this: dig it, or don't.

Sheet mulching

Although cultivating the soil is a time-honored method of preparing a bed for planting, this is not the only way to create a new garden. In fact, you can build a garden bed without digging. Really. Also known as lasagna gardening, no-till gardening, and sheet composting, the sheet mulching method of gardening eliminates the need to dig down by building up. With sheet mulching, you layer various types of organic materials (anything you would put in a compost bin) over the garden area—be it a raised bed, on top of existing soil, or on top of concrete. You can even use sheet mulching to convert an area of lawn to a veggie garden without enduring the painful task of ripping up sod. The layers eventually break down to create rich garden soil—essentially, this is composting in place.

Sheet mulching is a good method for creating new beds, because it eliminates the need to bring in costly soil; you can make your own incredibly fertile soil using stuff that would otherwise be considered trash. The major drawback to this technique is the time it takes for the layers to break down—sometimes more than a year. However, you can get around this hurdle by topping off your decomposing layers with several inches of quality soil and planting shallow-rooted crops. Another potential drawback is that sheet mulching raises the level of the soil, which may not suit your needs or taste.

o **Step one: prepare the site.** If the soil in the garden is not compacted, begin by cutting back any existing lawn or vegetation and marking the outline of your future garden. If your soil is compacted, begin by loosening it.

o **Step two: construct a frame (optional).** A frame isn't necessary, but it will help prevent soil loss through erosion. Place the frame in its final position.

o **Step three: lay down cardboard.** This is the first layer, upon which you will build your soil. This bottom layer should be plain (uncolored) cardboard with any tape and staples removed, or you can use multiple (ten or more) sheets of newspaper (choose sheets preferably without color ink). This layer will smother the grass or weeds below, so make sure you overlap the edges by at least 6 in. (15 cm) to prevent weeds from sneaking through. Water down this layer.

o **Step four: add a layer of carbon-rich organic matter.** Good sources of carbon tend to be brown, dry, or dead, such as straw, dry leaves, or wood chips. This layer should be about 6 in. (15 cm) deep.

o **Step five: add a layer of nitrogen-rich organic matter.** Nitrogen sources, such as unfinished compost, non-animal kitchen scraps, grass clippings, coffee grounds, and manure, tend to be green or wet. Add a thin layer, 2 to 3 in. (5 to 8 cm) deep.

o **Step six: repeat steps four and five.** Alternate layers of carbon-rich materials with layers of nitrogen-rich organic matter until your bed is about twice the desired height, ending with a layer of carbon.

o **Step seven: water.** Water the entire bed well to start the decomposition process. Keeping the bed moist over the coming months will also help the layers break down quickly. After watering and a few weeks of decomposition, the bed will have shrunk in height considerably.

o **Step eight: add soil.** Top the bed with a thick layer of compost or topsoil, about 4 in. (10 cm) deep.

o **Step nine: plant.** Ideally, you will build your sheet-mulched bed a year before you intend to plant, giving the materials ample time to break down. If you need to plant immediately, however, your best bet is to choose shallow-rooted plants such as lettuce greens and brassicas—at least for the first year.

· ·

Opposite: Got dirt? You've got options. And not all of them involve a shovel.

Tilling the soil

Although some gardeners almost never dig—because turning the soil can kill helpful microorganisms and damage soil structure—digging in organic matter is a good way to begin to repair soils that are compacted or otherwise lacking.

Next to sheet mulching, the simplest way to prepare a garden bed is to loosen your soil to a depth of about 6 to 10 in. (15 to 25 cm), incorporating compost or manure as you go. Or you could try a method of extreme soil preparation called double-digging, which is exactly that: double the digging. Sounds crazy—and it is a lot of work—but this technique is great for creating loose, deep, fertile soil that supports intensively planted crops.

The gist of double-digging is that you dig a trench about a foot (30 cm) deep, setting the displaced soil aside. Then dig down another foot, loosening that soil and amending it with organic matter. Dig another trench next to the first, piling the soil removed from it into the first trench (and again amending it with organic matter). Keep digging and amending, moving soil from trench to trench, breaking a mean sweat until your plot is well and truly aerated, fertilized, and loosened. The results last for years.

Removing sod (that is, grass or lawn) is also a bit of an ordeal. I am not advocating keeping your lawn, however—far from it. Just think about sheet mulching on top of your lawn instead of digging in, unless you're a big fan of blisters.

If you do need to remove sod, use a long-handled spade with a flat, sharp edge to cut the sod into sections. Then, using the spade like a pie lifter, jam it under a section of sod, slicing off the roots with the spade's sharp edge. Lift the sod away. Repeat with the other sections.

For removing large sections of lawn, consider renting a sod-cutting machine. Sod-cutters make quick work of this difficult job, and, if you don't mind building your bed up about 6 in. (15 cm), you can flip over the cut turf, spread a layer of compost on top, and plant into that. On the downside, the weight and vibrations of the sod-cutter in action will increase soil compaction (and, like all gas-powered machinery, contribute to air pollution), so be mindful of this when deciding whether to use one.

Opposite: Dry leaves make an excellent—and free—source of carbon for sheet mulching and composting.

PLANNING YOUR GARDEN

Think about your dream garden. What is growing there? Do you imagine stepping barefoot onto your deck to pluck sweet, juicy raspberries for your ice cream? Can you taste the crunch of fresh-picked sugar snap peas? Smell basil's spicy scent as you brush against it?

Everyone who imagines a garden has a few must-have plants in mind—those that say "summer!" or "dinner on the patio!" But the edibles you love may not love you back, and when you work within a small space, every plant must earn its place.

Opposite: A winter's evening spent dreaming about the coming summer soon turns into more fun than work.

As you decide what to grow, my hard-earned advice is this: resist the temptation to head off to the nursery and browse. It is too easy to drop a day's pay on seeds and seedlings, and then get home and realize you bought enough to start a small farm. So before you shell out for just one more pretty seed packet, do some planning. If you're not the organized type, this can be the toughest part of growing a food garden. But a certain level of planning is not only worth it, but mandatory. You will save money, get more out of your garden, and enjoy the process more if you take a few evenings to plan your garden before you plant.

WHAT SHOULD I GROW?

Make a list of everything you want to grow. If you have big dreams, make that list a long one. For now, don't let pesky details hold you back—such as the fact that rooftops are not usually considered appropriate places to grow wheat. If you want to grow it, put it on the list. Think about a few other things as well.

○ **Plant what you love to eat.** If you don't like squash, don't plant it simply because gardens are "supposed" to have squash or (and here's where I'm guilty) because it looks good on the seed package.

○ **Consider how you spend money at the grocery store.** For example, if you often pony up a few bucks a shot for those little plastic containers of herbs, you know herbs are a must grow.

○ **Note which edibles are hard to find in stores.** Unusual edibles such as sprouting broccoli are easy to grow at home. Think about choosing plants that are not available through mass-market retailers, such as heirloom fruits and vegetables.

○ **Remember what tastes best fresh from the garden.** All crops taste better fresh picked, but

some, such as corn, really aren't worth eating any other way.

○ **Know which fruits and vegetables, when conventionally grown, have the highest residual pesticide levels.** Consider crops from the "dirty dozen" list and slash your pesticide intake—and your grocery bill—by growing your own organics.

THE DIRTY DOZEN

Based on an analysis of nearly 96,000 tests for pesticide residues in produce conducted between 2000 and 2008 and collected by the U.S. government, researchers at the Environmental Working Group (www.ewg.org), a research and advocacy organization, have developed a list of 12 crops, called the dirty dozen—fruits and vegetables that consistently test higher for levels of pesticide residues. Here they are in descending order.

celery	blueberries	kale/collard greens
peaches	nectarines	cherries
strawberries	bell peppers	potatoes
apples	spinach	grapes (imported)

Source: "Shopper's Guide to Pesticides" (www.foodnews.org)

After you have created an impressive list, it's time to check in with reality and determine whether you can grow everything you want. Don't cross anything off your list just yet; you might decide to find another place to grow or perhaps wait until next year to try the crops that you don't plant this year.

Then ask yourself a few more questions.

○ **What will thrive in my space?** A plant might look great in someone else's garden, but will it grow in yours? Think about your site assessment and consider how your site conditions might affect what you can grow. For example, if your balcony gets only three hours of sunlight daily, you should look for another place to grow melons and other sun-lovers.

○ **Do I have time to look after it?** Although a small garden will not demand hours of tending every day, there is no such thing as a no-maintenance garden. Some crops, such as berries, spinach, peas, and beans, require almost daily harvesting for peak flavor and so they continue to produce—or because, like spinach, they go from up-and-coming to has-been in 3 seconds flat. Plant low-maintenance crops such as potatoes or perennial vegetables if your busy life tends to keep you away from the garden.

○ **What will be easy to grow?** Unless you are addicted to difficult relationships, avoid fussy crops when planting your first garden. Stick with beginner basics (see the "Top ten easiest edibles") until your thumbs green up, and you'll have a better chance at success—and you will be more likely to stick with it.

○ **Which edibles will produce the most amount of food in a limited space?** Artichokes are gorgeous plants (and so tasty with a bit of melted butter). But they are also enormous and may produce only one choke per plant. Do you really want to devote half your space to half a meal? Think about making the best use of limited space.

○ **What's good for my soil?** For a number of reasons, you should avoid planting the same crops in the same space year after year. Plants take the nutrients they need from the soil. If you plant the same thing in the same place repeatedly, those specific nutrients will eventually be exhausted. Just look at conventional agriculture's practice of mono-cropping to see the results: an ever-increasing reliance on chemical fertilizers. Crop rotation helps maintain healthy soil and plants.

A number of factors impact what you eventually plant and grow. One of the best ways to answer some of these questions is to have a basic knowledge of plant families.

. . . .

Opposite: Lettuce meets all my qualifications for a perfect crop. I use a lot of it, and it tastes best straight from the garden. It's also fast-growing, attractive, space-efficient, and easy to grow. Photo by Andrea Bellamy.

I have never been able to grow cilantro successfully, yet it is constantly touted as "easy to grow." Although a few crops are considered good beginner choices, don't get a complex if they fail to do well for you. Not all garden sites and situations work for all plants. That said, even a beginner—or anyone who would like a fighting chance at harvesting food this year—has some mighty fine choices.

beans	peas
beets	potatoes
chard	radishes
herbs	summer squash
lettuce and salad greens	tomatoes

Above: Beans are easy to grow and pretty, and they take up little space when grown vertically. They also return nitrogen to the soil.

PLANT FAMILIES

Thanks mostly to the work of Carolus Linnaeus, the father of modern taxonomy, every plant in your garden has been grouped with others that share several characteristics. If you think back to high school biology, you will remember that species, the smallest classification, falls under genus, which follows family, which follows order, class, phylum, and so on. In gardening, it helps to be aware of the first three: species, genus, and family.

Every plant has a Latin—or botanical—name made up of its genus and species names. A cultivar (cultivated variety) name is provided by a plant breeder and is often added to signify that the plant has been intentionally propagated by a breeder.

Common name	Botanical name		
	Genus	Species	Cultivar (cultivated variety)
Pineapple mint	*Mentha*	*suaveolens*	'Variegata'

Botanical names are used to describe plants because common names can vary from place to place. Although the name *Brassica oleracea* var. *botrytis* isn't used at the market (we call it cauliflower), its botanical name can tell us that it is related to *Brassica rapa* var. *rapa*, or turnip, even though these two vegetables seem quite different at first glance. *Brassica* is the shared genus name, *oleracea* and *rapa* are the respective species names, and var. *botrytis* and var. *rapa* are the varietal names. In this case, the botanical name tells us that both cauliflower and turnip are members of the brassica family. (This is not always the case with genus names, however; usually, the genus name differs from the family name.)

So what? Well, because we know cauliflower and turnip are brassicas, we can surmise many things about their soil and climate preferences, potential pests and diseases, the way they flower and set seed, and what we could plant beside them for best results. Like human families, plant relatives share characteristics and preferences—and knowing a bit about them can help us grow them more successfully.

Knowledge of plant families is also useful when you are planning for crop rotation—the practice of alternating what you grow on a particular plot of land from season to season or year to year. Plants from the same family deplete the soil of similar nutrients. Planting the same crop family in the same place year after year can also cause the pathogens and pests that prey on that family to build up in the soil. By rotating the crop families you plant in a space, you can avoid all that nastiness.

Group families of edibles together when you are planning your garden. At this point in the planning process, I like to take my list of edibles and note the crop family for each. This information will help me decide where, when, and how to plant each crop.

Of the hundreds of plant families, a few are most important for food gardeners to know.

· ·

Below: Alliums, such as onions, make good companion plants to many other vegetables because of their pest-repelling qualities.

The alliums (Alliaceae)

Thank goodness for alliums. Not only do chives, garlic, leeks, onions, scallions (green onions), and shallots play a crucial role in cookery, but their aromatic qualities offer pest protection to other crops, making them excellent companion plants in the garden.

○ **Climate:** Alliums are cool-season crops that prefer the damp, cool weather of spring and fall.

○ **Soil:** Most alliums are not fussy—just give them relatively fertile soil with good drainage.

○ **Good companions:** Alliums actually repel many pests because of their aromatic properties, making them a friend to crops that are susceptible to slugs and other leaf-eating pests. They are, however, susceptible to mildew and fungal infections, often caused by poorly draining soil or humid conditions during hot weather. Following an infected planting of alliums with brassicas can reduce mildew in the soil.

The amaranths (Amaranthaceae)

The amaranths are nutritious, delicious, and some of the most beautiful edibles you will ever grow. The amaranth family is a cool-season group of leaf and root crops that includes protein-rich grains amaranth and quinoa, container-friendly cousins beet (or beetroot) and chard (also known as Swiss chard and silverbeet), and versatile spinach.

○ **Climate:** Amaranths are at their peak during the cool weather of spring and fall. Some will bolt (produce seeds rather than the leaves or roots we like) in the heat of summer, but many will happily weather winter's worst.

○ **Soil:** Good soil preparation is key to growing these crops. They prefer fertile, moist, well-drained soil that is rich in organic matter.

○ **Good companions:** Umbellifers such as fennel help to attract beneficial insects that prey on leaf miners and other pests that plague members of Amaranthaceae. Alliums and other aromatics repel slugs and other bandits.

The brassicas (Brassicaceae)

The family Brassicaceae is huge and diverse and includes arugula (rocket), Asian greens, broccoli, Brussels sprouts, cabbage, cauliflower, Chinese cabbage, collards, kale, kohlrabi, mizuna, mustard, radishes, rutabagas, and turnips—to name a few.

○ **Climate:** Another family in the cool-and-damp camp, some brassicas bolt in hot weather. Many will easily overwinter, becoming sweeter after cold weather and frost. Their insectary flowers (attractive to beneficial insects) are edible.

○ **Soil:** With so much diversity, a brassica is available for every soil type. They tend to prefer moist, well-drained, fertile, slightly alkaline soil with plenty of organic matter.

○ **Good companions:** Brassicas play nice with most other families, bringing pollinators to the garden with their flowers and helping alliums battle mildew. Interplant with aromatics to discourage pests.

Opposite: Cabbage, a brassica, stands out against a leafy backdrop of potatoes, members of the nightshade family.

CROP ROTATION STRATEGIES

Most crop rotation plans are based on a three- or four-year cycle and can look similar to this chart.

	Bed one	Bed two	Bed three
Year 1	root crops	legumes	brassicas
Year 2	legumes	brassicas	root crops
Year 3	brassicas	root crops	legumes

This is not the only way to manage crop rotations, however. Other common planting plans include rotating potatoes, brassicas, legumes, and root crops; legumes, onions/carrots/tomatoes, and brassicas; heavy feeders, light feeders, and soil builders; and roots, brassicas, and other crops.

Crop rotation need not occur on a multiple-year basis, either. Within a single growing year, you could harvest overwintered cabbages (brassicas) in spring, and then plant a main crop of potatoes (nightshades, root crop), followed by a fall cover crop of broad beans (legumes).

The basic idea is to rotate crops that are heavy feeders (such as brassicas and tomatoes) with light feeders (such as umbellifers and alliums), nutrient builders (such as legumes), and crops that improve soil structure (such as potatoes).

If it all seems too complicated, remember that no hard-and-fast rules govern crop rotation, and your garden will not be a total flop if you grow the same edibles in the same spot for more than a single year. Just be conscious of the principles behind crop rotation and try to practice it when possible. It will result in better yields and fewer pests—which is enough of an incentive for most gardeners.

The cucurbits (Cucurbitaceae)

The cucurbit family contains garden favorites cucumber, melon, pumpkin, squash, and zucchini. This warm-season group of annual bushes and vines have hairy stems and large, edible flowers. Many can be trained up trellises or along railings, making them great small-space producers.

- **Climate:** These tropical natives love warm temperatures and lots of sun. (Can you blame them?)

- **Soil:** Fertile, moist, well-drained soil is a must.

- **Good companions:** The cucurbits' broad leaves provide great shade for heat-shy plants and shield the soil, preventing surface evaporation. Their spiny stems and leaves repel many pests and are traditionally used to keep raccoons and squirrels out of corn patches.

The legumes (Fabaceae)

The legume family includes peas, lentils, peanuts, snap beans, soybeans, and broad beans. In addition to the tasty seedpods and seeds produced by legumes, they are useful in the garden because they fix nitrogen in the soil via a symbiotic relationship with bacteria. The bacteria attaches to the plants' roots as small nodules, turning nitrogen pulled from the air into useable nitrogen for the plant, and releasing it into the soil when the plant dies.

- **Climate:** From cool-season (and even overwintering) choices such as peas and broad beans, to warm-season crops such as pole beans, this family thrives in a wide range of climates.

- **Soil:** Legumes are fairly easy-going as long as the soil is well drained.

- **Good companions:** Because of their relationship with nitrogen-fixing bacteria, legumes will improve nitrogen levels in your soil, making them an excellent choice to plant with, or prior to, crops that benefit from high nitrogen. Legumes play a crucial role in crop rotation and cover cropping for this reason.

. . . .

Right: Whether snap, snow, or shelling, all peas are members of the legume family and are related to beans and peanuts.

Opposite: Potatoes are one of the easiest nightshades to grow, tolerating a range of climates and soil conditions.

The nightshades (Solanaceae)

If you automatically think, *deadly* when you hear the word *nightshade*, there is good reason for that. Solanaceae contain varying levels of a mild toxin known as belladonna. Even so, this family includes such kitchen staples as tomatoes, potatoes, eggplants, and hot and sweet peppers. Belladonna is mainly found in the flowers, leaves, and stalks, which humans have largely learned to avoid—except for one of the most deadly nightshade crops: tobacco.

- **Climate:** With the exception of the humble potato, which can be grown just about anywhere, nightshades do best in hot, sunny conditions.

- **Soil:** Nightshades are fairly easygoing when it comes to soil, although they dislike heavy soils with poor drainage.

- **Good companions:** Any pollinator-attracting, pest-repelling plant is a friend to nightshades. Aromatic herbs such as basil and oregano are traditionally planted with tomatoes to improve the flavor of the fruit.

The umbellifers (Apiaceae)

The old botanical name for this family is Umbel-liferae. Umbellifer has the same root as the word umbrella, which this family's flowers resemble. Carrots, celery, dill, fennel, parsley, and parsnips are members. In addition to being good eating, they have tremendous value in the garden as insectary (beneficial insect-attracting) plants.

○ **Climate:** Like alliums and brassicas, umbel-lifers are a cool-season crop, with some members being among the most cold-hardy edibles. They prefer full sun.

○ **Soil:** Although most umbellifers do not require especially fertile soil, they grow best in soil that is loose and well-drained. Most are intolerant of acidic soil.

○ **Good companions:** Because of their aromatic and insectary properties, umbellifers are great companions to any crop that benefits from the pollinators they attract and the pests they repel. Nightshades are a classic companion.

. . . .

Opposite: With its wide range of culinary uses, attractive form, and tolerance for many growing conditions, parsley is one of the most commonly grown umbellifers.

COOL-SEASON VERSUS WARM-SEASON VEGETABLES

Cool-season vegetables enjoy the cool, damp weather of early spring, and often late summer and autumn as well. Some will even survive frost, and in areas with mild winters they can be harvested all winter long. In contrast, warm-season vegetables need heat and longer days to produce and ripen fruit. Being sensitive to cold, they must be planted out well after the spring's last frost.

In climates with short growing seasons, growing warm-season vegetables can be challenging. Look for vegetables with a low number of "days to maturity" (which will be noted on the seed packet), to ensure that your plants have time to ripen before the weather turns cool.

ANNUALS, BIENNIALS, AND PERENNIALS

Families are only one way of classifying plants. One of the most basic distinctions for all plants is whether they are annual, biennial, or perennial.

As the name suggests, annual edibles are planted and harvested all within one year. The majority of common vegetable crops are annuals or are grown as annuals.

Unlike annuals, perennials return year after year without much—if any—help from you. Asparagus and rhubarb are the most commonly grown perennial vegetables in temperate climate gardens, but dozens of less well-known perennial vegetables are worthy of garden space. Fruit trees and shrubs are perennial, as are several herbs. They last for years—even decades—and once established tend to require little maintenance.

Biennials plants such as carrots, onions, cabbage, parsley, and beets take two years to complete their lifecycle. Plant them one year, harvest their crops the same year, but collect their seeds the next. Knowing which plants are biennials is relevant only if you want to save the seeds they produce. Because saving and planting the seeds of biennial plants can be a little complicated, most gardeners treat them as annuals, buying and planting new seeds each year.

....

Below: Plant climbing vines, such as this 'Suyo Long' cucumber, against a railing, trellis, or other support structure. Photo by Andrea Bellamy.

Opposite: Trees and woody shrubs such as gooseberry are long-lived perennials.

WHERE AND WHEN TO PLANT

After you understand the needs and preferences of the plants on your list, it's time to find a place for them in your garden.

Where to plant

If you have an in-ground garden or use large containers for your garden, you can plant edibles from compatible families together. Even if they are planted in separate containers, many complementary plants will perform better if their containers are grouped together.

I like to sketch out my garden—which is essentially a collection of containers of various sizes—and assign plants (based on plant family, space and sun requirements, and other needs) to each container.

When you are deciding where to plant, or to place your containers, keep a few things in mind.

o **Height.** How tall will this plant grow? If you plant it in front of a shorter edible, it may grow to shade the smaller plant (which may or may not be a bad thing, depending on the shaded plant). Some edibles, such as amaranths and lettuces, like a little shade in hot weather.

o **Sun.** How much sun does the plant need? If your outdoor space offers varying levels of sunshine, place sun-lovers where they can take advantage of the greatest amount of sunshine, and put shade-tolerant edibles in areas that receive less sun.

o **Support.** Will the plant require support, or can it be grown upward for the greatest use of space? Vine tomatoes usually need staking to keep them from keeling over. Peas, pole beans, and some cucurbits can be grown up trellises or other supports to make the most of vertical space. Position these plants to take advantage of railings or walls that could act as supports.

o **Shelter.** Is the plant prone to rain-induced blights or diseases? If your growing area is sheltered by a roof overhang or other shelter, situate your tomatoes and cucurbits underneath to help them stay clear of blight and powdery mildew. If your balcony or rooftop is prone to heavy winds, place plants with delicate foliage in the shelter of windbreaks.

When to plant

As in cooking, timing is everything when it comes to planting your garden. Plant too early in the season and your seeds may rot in the cold, wet soil—or they may simply fail to germinate because of the chilly weather. Plant too late and the cool fall weather may arrive before your plants have had time to set fruit.

To organize your planting schedule for the year, take a look at your list of edibles and note when each one should be planted, indicating whether you will sow seeds or transplant seedlings (either bought from the nursery or raised from seed indoors). Seed starting dates can be found on the seed packets. (The example table shown below is for North American planting based on the last frost date of March 28.)

This is a great way to keep track of your planting dates. Plug these dates into your calendar, and you won't miss your window for planting.

. . . .

Opposite: Tomatoes need plenty of sun to be truly productive. On this rooftop deck, they sunbathe in front of solar panels.

EDIBLE	DAYS TO HARVEST	WHEN TO PLANT	START INDOORS?
Beet, 'Chioggia'	65	mid-April to July	No (direct sow)
Broccoli, 'Everest'	50	April	Yes, in March
Carrot, 'Thumbelina'	60	mid-April to July	No (direct sow)
Cucumber, 'Lemon'	70	June	Yes, in May

A	EARLY to MIDSPRING	LATE SPRING to EARLY SUMMER	MIDSUMMER to EARLY FALL	MIDFALL to LATE WINTER
PLANT	Beets, broccoli, carrots	Beets, broccoli, carrots, cucumber	Beets, carrots	
HARVEST		Beets, broccoli, carrots	Beets, broccoli, carrots, cucumber	Carrots

B	EARLY to MIDSPRING	LATE SPRING to EARLY SUMMER	MIDSUMMER to EARLY FALL	MIDFALL to LATE WINTER
PLANT	Arugula, beets, broccoli, carrots, radishes	Beets, broccoli, carrots, cucumber	Arugula, beets, broad beans, carrots, garlic, radishes	
HARVEST	Arugula, radishes	Arugula, beets, broccoli, carrots, radishes	Arugula, beets, broccoli, carrots, cucumber, radishes	Arugula, carrots, radishes

I also like to create a simple chart outlining what I will plant and harvest across the seasons. This can help you recognize any obvious empty spots so that you can modify your planting list to ensure a year-round harvest. In example A, nothing is being harvested during the spring.

If arugula and radishes were added to the list, they could be planted and harvested within the season, as shown in example B. Add an overwintering edible such as broad beans or garlic to your midsummer planting to ensure that you'll have something to harvest next spring or summer, too.

If you're not a planner by nature, all this work up front can seem daunting and perhaps even over-complicated. But with good planning, you will realize the rewards when you reap the bounty of a healthy, productive edible garden. Do your planning early in the season before you feel rushed to start getting things in the ground—and, above all, enjoy the process.

Opposite: Patty Pan squash is a warm-season vegetable.

GETTING DIRTY

Ah, soil. Seemingly the most mundane of topics, bring it up in conversation and keen organic gardeners will be talking for hours. But there is good reason for their excitement. Soil is the primary factor in the success of your garden.

It took me a long time to appreciate soil. I wasn't squeamish about worms or bugs, or precious about getting dirt under my nails; I never really considered what soil did for us—it was just something plants grew in.

I grew up gardening alongside my parents and grandparents—experienced gardeners all. But in the early years of gardening on my own, I went through the motions of making compost and mulching, knowing that it was what I was *supposed* to do. It wasn't until I took the time to learn about soil that I grasped *why* I was doing it.

Opposite: Healthy soils are dark, rich, and full of organic matter.

Soil doesn't simply hold plants—it supports them. Thus, it is our job as organic gardeners to support the soil and the myriad life forms that exist within it (which, in turn, help feed our plants). This might seem obvious, but it's amazing how much time and effort we put into choosing containers, building plant supports, fussing over weeds or aphids, trimming, tidying, and puttering about the garden—all while neglecting the most important element.

WHAT IS SOIL?

Soil is made up of minerals (eroded rock) and organic matter (decaying and well-decayed plant and animal matter, as well as living creatures such as worms and microorganisms).

Healthy soil is dark, rich, and crumbly. It smells sweet and, well, earthy. It is teeming with life: earthworms and insects, as well as fungi, bacteria, and other microorganisms. Although mineral content is important, the living part of the soil fuels plant growth.

Soil organisms act as decomposers, breaking down organic matter and turning it into nutrients plants can use. Without these organisms, plants cannot take up the nutrients they need to thrive. Worms are also decomposers that carry leaf litter and other surface-level debris deeper into the soil, leaving behind nutrient-rich castings (worm poo) and aerating the soil in the process.

"Dead" soil lacks organic matter, including these crucial organisms. Urban soils, particular those in new developments, are often dry, dusty, and completely bereft of nutrients: they are essentially dead. But, thankfully, even the worst soils can be remediated.

THE ORGANIC APPROACH

Organic growers look at soil as the critical element to a successful garden. Healthy soil grows healthy plants that are stronger, more productive, and better able to fight off diseases and pests. This is why many organic gardeners think about gardening in terms of growing the soil (rather than the plants). In contrast, the nonorganic approach uses chemical fertilizers that provide a short-term boost to plants but do nothing to improve the soil. In fact, chemical fertilizers and pesticides may actually harm the soil by disrupting the natural balance of soil-dwelling organisms.

SOIL ORGANIC MATTER: YOUR NEW BEST FRIEND

If this chapter has a common theme, it is that organic matter is the key to healthy soil. Organic matter is the part of the soil that's alive—not just with microbes, bacteria, and other helpful organisms, but also with well-decayed and decaying plant and animal matter, which provides the fuel for these nutrient recyclers.

Soil organic matter neutralizes the effects of wonky pH, improves soil structure and airflow, increases a soil's water-holding capacity while improving drainage, and provides the main source of nutrients for plants.

Is there anything organic matter cannot do? Actually, no. If you were to add nothing else to your garden but a good source of organic matter, such as compost, manure, worm castings, or leaf mulch, your garden would be happy. Luckily, organic matter is easy to come by, and, best of all, it's free.

Opposite: Healthy soil produces healthy plants. Building healthy soil is job one for organic gardeners.

Soil pH

Soil pH indicates the acidity or alkalinity of your soil on a scale of 1 to 14, with 7.0 being neutral. A pH lower than 7.0 indicates an acidic soil, and a pH greater than 7.0 indicates an alkaline soil. Most plants prefer soil that is neutral to slightly acidic, although exceptions exist. If your soil is very acidic or very alkaline, most plants will suffer. In such soils, plants have difficulty accessing nutrients, leading to deficiencies and poor health. You can test the pH of your soil using a kit obtained from a garden center or by sending a soil sample to a lab.

○ **Acid soils.** Most edible plants grow well in acid soil. Some, such as blueberries or potatoes, demand it. If, however, your soil is too acidic (drop below pH 5.5 and many crops will protest), you can add lime as needed. Lime has the added benefit of supplying calcium to the soil. Follow the application instructions on the box; if in doubt, go for a light touch. Wood ash can also be used to raise the pH of acid soils. Mix it with water before applying, and be careful not to inhale the dust.

○ **Alkaline soils.** Brassicas prefer a slightly alkaline soil, but a pH above 7.2 doesn't suit most other crops. Sulfur is commonly sold as a quick-fix amendment for acidifying alkaline soils, but coffee grounds and pine needles also work, though more slowly.

ADJUSTING SOIL PH

The best way to improve acid or alkaline soils is to add organic matter—such as compost, leaf mulch, or manure. Organic matter has a buffering ability—to self-regulate pH—that acts by holding onto excess minerals and nutrients so they don't tip the balance. For this reason, most plants growing in soil high in organic matter will do just fine—even if the pH is a point or more away from ideal.

Opposite: Potatoes prefer an acidic soil with a pH below 6.0. Most vegetables will do well in soil with a pH of 6.0 to 7.2.

Soil texture

You might have heard gardeners complain about soil that is pure clay or mostly sand—they are talking about soil texture. Texture refers to the mineral content of the soil—specifically, the size of the mineral particles in the soil and their relative proportion to one another.

Particles are classified by size, from smallest to largest, as clay, silt, and sand. The larger the particle size, the larger the air pockets (known as pores) between them. Pores allow water and air to move through the soil, which is why sandy soils drain quickly and clay soils tend to become hard and waterlogged. Silt falls somewhere between the two.

The ultimate goal for most gardeners is a soil with roughly equal proportions of sand, silt, and clay—along with a healthy dose of organic matter. This results in a magical substance called loam, and this is what you want in your garden.

Loam is more nutrient-rich than sand and drains better than silt and clay. It retains water, yet doesn't become waterlogged. In short, loam is the perfect soil for growing food. Luckily, you can create loam even in sandy or clay-heavy soils. It takes time and work, but by regularly adding organic matter such as compost and/or manure, your soil will gradually tip toward the center of the texture scale.

○ **Sandy soils.** Sandy soils have two major drawbacks: they lack nutrients and organic matter (which go hand-in-hand), and they do not hold moisture. The solution to both issues is to add in tons of organic matter—compost, manure, or leaf mulch, for example—every spring and fall.

Poor urban soils often pass for sandy, but these soils are frequently made up of construction debris and grit and are just as nutrient-poor as sand. The solution is the same: add organic matter, which will allow the soil to hold water and improve its structure and nutrient content.

Or, if this all seems like too much work, plant carrots—they enjoy sandy soil, because it allows their roots to develop freely. Drought-tolerant Mediterranean herbs such as thyme, oregano, rosemary, and sage also tolerate sandy soils.

○ **Clay soils.** Clay soils don't drain well, offer little porosity for air and water circulation, and tend to become hard and compacted. The only good news is that they hold nutrients well. Dig in organic matter—lots of it—as well as sand or horticultural grit to improve porosity and drainage.

Potatoes will help to break up clay soils, but forget about planting other root crops such as carrots or parsnips. Since clay soils tend to take longer to warm up in spring, choose mid- to late-season crops, and avoid crops that demand great drainage, such as Mediterranean herbs.

Soil structure

Together with texture, soil structure has a huge impact on plant health. Soil structure refers to how soil particles clump together. These clumps of soil, which can be tiny or large, are called aggregates. The best soils have a variety of aggregate sizes and shapes, which allows space for the movement of water, air, roots, and organisms.

The greatest threat to soil structure is compaction. When humans or machines move over soil, it becomes compressed, and clay soils are particularly prone to this. Compaction reduces air circulation and a soil's ability to absorb and filter water, so avoid stepping on your garden beds when possible.

TESTING YOUR SOIL

You can use many kinds of tests to check your soil. You can use do-it-yourself kits, available at your local garden center, to determine your soil's pH or nutrient content, or soil labs can perform detailed analyses of the mineral content and makeup of your soil. These tests can be fun in a science fair kind of way, but they are not strictly necessary. You can tell a lot about your soil by getting up close and personal with it.

Dig up a spadeful of soil and take a good look. How many worms can you see? How many mites and millipedes? Soil hopping with all kinds of organisms is a pretty good indicator that your soil is high in organic matter—the foundation of all healthy soils.

If you want to get a little more scientific and learn about the texture of your soil, you can use two easy do-it-yourself testing methods. Both begin with a soil sample.

Collecting a soil sample

Brush any loose mulch or leaf debris from the surface of your soil. Use a trowel to dig a hole 4 to 6 in. deep (10 to 15 cm); set this soil aside. Next, using your trowel, scrape or cut a thin slice of soil from the side of the hole. Place this soil in a clean container. Repeat in spots throughout the area you want to test, and add the soil from these additional locations to the initial soil sample. Mix well.

The texture-by-feel test

Take a small, moist handful of soil in your hands and work it: roll it, rub it, and get a good feel for it. Soil with a heavy ratio of sand will feel (and even sound) gritty and rough and will not stick together to form a ball. Silt feels smooth and floury, but not as elastic as clay. Clay-based soils feel sticky when wet, look shiny, and will not only form a nice solid ball but could probably be thrown on a wheel and turned into a vase.

. . . .

Opposite: Dig up at least one worm in a spadeful of soil, and you know your garden is in pretty good shape.

Right: Layers of sand, silt, and clay are visible after being left to settle for a few days.

The soil-in-a-jar test

Add a cup (237 ml) of your soil sample to a roughly 2 pint (1 L) jar, having removed any rocks or large bits of organic matter. Mix in a tablespoon (15 ml) of powdered dishwasher detergent (the soap acts as a surfactant, allowing for a more accurate reading). Then fill the jar with water, screw on the lid, and shake it thoroughly. Set the jar aside and forget about it for a few days. Do not disturb it during this time, because the particles need time to settle.

The bigger the particles, the faster they will settle in the jar. Sand, being the largest, falls fastest and will settle almost immediately at the bottom of the jar. Silt, the second largest particle type, should look darker and less coarse than the sand layer. It will settle out within a few hours. The last to settle will be clay, the smallest particles in the mix. These particles should be lighter-colored than those of silt and can take several days to settle. Measure the layers with a ruler to determine the makeup of your soil. So, for example, if you have 2 in. (5 cm) of sand, 1/2 in. (1 cm) of silt, and just a sprinkling of clay, you know your soil is made up of mostly sand, with a bit of silt. Soil scientists call this "loamy sand."

SOIL FOR CONTAINERS

Container garden soils are by necessity different from soils of in-ground gardens. If you put garden soil in containers—even if it started out rich and healthy—it would soon become hard and compact, suffocating your plants' roots.

Soil for containers, known as potting soil or simply container soil, is lighter than standard garden soil and is designed to provide the drainage and air circulation container-grown plants need.

The name potting soil is kind of misleading, because standard potting soil contains very little—if any—actual soil. Instead, it comprises a variety of organic and inorganic materials that contribute various qualities to the mix, such as good drainage and moisture and nutrient retention.

Classic soilless potting mixes are usually made up of large quantities of peat moss combined with perlite (white, lightweight, puffed volcanic rock added to improve drainage), vermiculite (a heated mineral product that looks like fish scales, added to improve water-holding capacity), and/or sand (which also improves drainage).

Because they contain no soil, these traditional potting mixes lack the living organisms that carry out the nutrient cycling that makes living soil function. And because microorganisms aren't doing the work of feeding the soil, you have to do it yourself. Mix in your own homemade compost or a granular complete organic fertilizer when planting. A biweekly liquid feed with a balanced organic fertilizer will also help keep things growing.

You can also purchase organic soil-based potting soils; they usually contain compost, along with soil conditioners such as coir or perlite. Some excellent soil-based products are on the market—ask for a

recommendation at a trusted garden center. Because these types of potting soils contain nutrient-rich compost, you won't have to fertilize quite so often.

Many gardeners custom blend their own potting soils using a mix of coir or peat, perlite, compost, and other soil amendments—but storing all those products is a challenge in small spaces. There is no shame in simply ripping open a bag of good quality potting soil.

Make sure you look for something labeled organic "container mix" or "potting soil"—do not buy topsoil. If in doubt, ask someone at a garden center you trust for a premium organic potting soil or container mix. Good retailers will give you honest appraisals of the potting mixes they sell.

PEAT

Peat, or sphagnum, moss is a common ingredient in potting soil mixes. It acts like a sponge, holding water but draining freely. It's lightweight and holds nutrients well. It has a slightly acidic pH. Despite these positives, I do not recommend using peat because it is mined from ecologically sensitive bogs and wetlands. Look for a peat alternative such as coir, instead. Coir is made from coconut hulls and is a sustainable peat substitute. Although it has little nutrient value, like peat it holds moisture well, lightens the soil, and promotes good air circulation.

Opposite: Containers need specially blended soil that is designed to promote good air circulation and drainage.

COMPOST

Making and using compost is simply the best thing you can do for your garden—not to mention the fact that it diverts a huge amount of waste away from the landfill. Use compost as a mulch (spread it on top of the soil to keep weeds down, reduce evaporation and erosion, and build up soil nutrients), combine it with potting soil to create a killer container mix, or add a handful to planting holes before transplanting shrubs or seedlings.

Composting can happen anywhere: in an open pile in the back corner of your yard, in a bin designed especially for composting, in a box under your sink, or even in a planter on your deck. Successful compost requires air, moisture, and a good balance of organic waste materials.

How to make compost

Making compost is quite easy once you understand a few key guidelines. Successful, nonstinky compost is made using a mixture of green stuff (wet, nitrogen-rich matter such as grass clippings and kitchen scraps) and brown stuff (dry, carbon-rich matter such as dead leaves and straw). Aim for a ratio of at least twice as much browns to greens.

When building compost, start with a layer of brown matter. I like to use a thick layer (about 6 in., or 15 cm) of chopped up twigs and branches for the first layer; this allows for good air circulation at the bottom of the bin. Follow this with a layer of green matter. Throw in a bucketful of compost (kindly donated by a neighbor or gardener friend) to jumpstart your compost by introducing worms, bacteria, and other helpful decomposers. Keep alternating layers of greens and browns, not necessarily all at once, until your bin is full or you run out of materials. Try to finish with a layer of browns—exposed greens tend to attract pests.

Turn your compost (mix it up) at least several times a year, adding water if necessary (compost should be slightly damp, like a wrung-out sponge). Air circulation speeds up the process of decomposition and prevents the compost pile from becoming stagnant. Depending on the size of your pile (larger piles heat up faster and thus finish more quickly), you can expect finished compost—rich, crumbly black humus—within a couple of months to a year.

Where to make compost

Making compost is a no-brainer if you have lots of outdoor space. Unfortunately, most of us are not so lucky. But even if you are gardening on a balcony, you can usually find a place to make usable compost.

- **In an open pile.** Building an unenclosed compost pile is the easiest way to make compost (and I'm all for low effort). Just pile up your greens and browns and let them sit. Turn the pile if you feel like it. If your pile is large enough, it will generate heat and "cook" its contents, providing high-quality compost in no time. An open pile is great if you have a tucked-away space and understanding neighbors. The downside to an open pile is that it looks messy and can attract pests—be they rodents, raccoons, or the dog next door.

- **In a bin.** Dozens of ready-made compost bins are available and range from simple wooden constructions to circular plastic units designed for easy turning. They are almost always built with holes or slats to facilitate air circulation, and with flaps or doors near the bottom for removing the finished compost. Bins keep things tidy, help insulate your compost (which speeds up its decomposition), and protect its tasty morsels from foraging critters.

Many store-bought compost bins have open bottoms, which can make them challenging to use on a patio or balcony. Look for a style with an enclosed bottom and set it on slats or blocks over a tray (some holes will be in the bottom for aeration, so some liquid will escape). You can make your own bin using a plastic garbage can, drilling holes around the sides and bottom. If you use a round container, you can aerate the contents by tipping it on its side (lid on) and rolling it back and forth.

- **As you go.** Cut out the middleman by disposing of your kitchen and garden scraps in the spot you want to enrich. Using this composting in-place method, you can create good soil by burying kitchen scraps (chopping up larger pieces) in a hole or trench in the garden or at the bottom of a large container. Bury the scraps with the soil you just removed. If you're adding scraps to a container, add

....

Opposite: Full of worms and microorganisms, compost is the ideal amendment for any soil.

a thick layer (6 in., or 15 cm) of garden or potting soil on top to prevent the scraps from smelling and attracting pests.

○ **In a worm bin.** Vermicomposting uses worms to turn your kitchen waste into quality compost. For gardeners without space for conventional composting, vermicomposting is the way to go. It takes little room; worms will live happily in a bin under your kitchen sink. If you don't have room indoors for a bin of 1 to 3 ft. (30 to 90 cm) wide and long, rethink the worm bin; worms should be protected from freezing temperatures, as well as temperatures above 86°F (30°C).

You can buy worm composters online, in garden centers, or even through forward-thinking city governments. You can also make your own by drilling holes into the lid, bottom, and sides of a plastic or wooden bin.

Worm bins need three ingredients to get started: bedding for the worms (dampened, shredded newspaper works well), a scoop of garden soil to add grit and beneficial microorganisms, and worms of course! Don't use earthworms from your garden; instead, track down red wigglers or brandling worms, (*Eisenia foetida*)—superstar composters that can be found at bait shops and garden centers. They like tight spaces and eat their way through a lot more waste than do common garden worms.

If you lack space for a bin or a worm composter, think about asking your landlord if you can start one on your building's common property. My compost bin lives in the alley just outside my gate, and I share it with a neighbor.

. . . .

Opposite, clockwise from top left: Cut up twigs and small-diameter branches so that they will break down faster. // Dry leaves are an excellent source of carbon, and they keep your compost from becoming too wet—and smelly. // Compost bins are not all that attractive, so look for an out-of-the-way spot, build a screen, or plant bright flowers—such as nasturtiums—to distract the eye (photo by Andrea Bellamy). // You can buy special bins for holding kitchen waste until you have time to visit the compost pile—this one has a carbon filter in the lid to block odors. Ice cream buckets and large yogurt containers can also be used.

Right: Shredded newspaper acts as worm bedding and should be replaced regularly as it breaks down.

WHAT TO COMPOST

You can compost a whole bunch of things beyond vegetable scraps and leaves. Compostables are classified as green or brown: Green matter is wet and nitrogen-rich. Browns are dry and carbon-rich. For example, grass clippings are considered green when fresh and still wet, but brown when they're dry and dead.

BROWNS

dry plant matter—dead leaves, stalks, twigs, and grass

straw or hay

shredded newspaper or cardboard

paper towels

sawdust

wood chips

pine needles

wood ashes

wine corks

GREENS

uncooked fruit and veggie scraps

washed eggshells

coffee grounds and teabags

fresh grass clippings, leaves, and plant matter

manure

weeds that have not gone to seed

hair (your pet's or yours, if it hasn't been chemically treated)

seaweed

DO NOT COMPOST

meat or fish

cooked food

fat or oil

dog or cat feces

diseased plants

perennial weeds or weeds that have gone to seed

MULCH

After composting, mulching is the next best thing you can do for your soil. (And you can combine the two by mulching with compost!) Mulching is the practice of spreading a layer of material (known as mulch) over the surface of your soil. Mulch comes in many forms. Traditional mulches include straw, compost, leaf mold (leaf compost), and bark mulch, but plastic sheeting, cardboard and newspaper, pebbles, and even fabric can be used as well.

Mulching protects the soil from erosion, reduces evaporation, and acts as an insulator to protect plants' roots in winter and to moderate the effects of hot summer temperatures. Using attractive mulches can give your containers or beds a freshly planted look. But where mulch really shines is in weed control; it can keep even the most persistent weeds at bay.

If you use nutrient-rich organic mulch (compost or leaf mold rather than cardboard or plastic sheeting, for example), it will not only provide all the described benefits, but it will also act as a soil amendment, because, over time, its nutritional goodness will be carried into the soil by earthworms and microbes.

Spread a layer between 2 and 4 in. (5 and 10 cm) thick over the exposed surfaces of your soil. The mulch should not touch the stem or trunk of a plant; leave a little breathing room. Mulch that sits against stems and stalks traps moisture and can encourage disease and rot.

Green mulches

Another type of mulch is different enough from the rest to warrant its own category. Green mulches, also known as living mulches or green manure, are living plants chosen specifically for the nutrients and structure they return to the soil after they are cut down and allowed to decompose.

Green mulches are grown as a cover crop; they cover the soil like mulch, and, like all mulches, they suppress weeds and prevent erosion. You can plant green mulch in any garden space that is not going to be planted for a month or more. I like to plant green mulches in fall for use in the winter garden.

Cover cropping with a green mulch does double—make that triple—duty in the winter garden. First, it protects your soil from harsh winter weather, preventing erosion, compaction, and nutrient leaching. Second, many popular green mulches fix nitrogen in the soil. I could go into a whole scientific explanation behind the "fixing" of nitrogen, but all you really need to know is that these plants, many of which are nitrogen-fixing clovers and legumes, take nitrogen from the air and make it available in the soil, prepping soil for spring planting. And readily available nitrogen is a great service to soil that has been depleted by hungry feeders such as tomatoes or corn. Finally, green mulches improve soil structure by adding organic matter when the mulch is tilled or dug into the soil.

In the spring, either dig under the green mulch crop and mix it into the soil, or cut it down, leaving the roots in the ground and using the greens for your compost. If you dig it under, let the soil rest for three weeks before planting. Then enjoy improved soil fertility and structure.

Popular nitrogen-fixing green mulches include pretty red clover (*Trifolium pratense*), Austrian field pea (*Pisum sativum*), and fava bean (*Vicia faba*). Combine one or more of these legumes with a grass or cereal such as winter rye (*Secale cereale*), common oats (*Avena sativa*), or common wheat (*Triticum aestivum*), which improve soil structure and add organic matter once tilled under.

. . . .

Opposite, clockwise from top left: Straw mulch suppresses weeds, prevents soil erosion and water evaporation, and keeps developing fruit out of direct contact with the soil. // Compost is the best mulch around. It not only suppresses weeds and limits evaporation, but it feeds the soil as its nutrients are carried in by worms and microbes. // Blades of winter rye poke through among hardy vegetables (photo by Andrea Bellamy). // Because it helps warm the soil, black plastic mulch is commonly used with plants that produce better in warmer temperatures. It is also an effective weed barrier.

OTHER SOIL SUPPLEMENTS

I used to think that being an organic gardener meant avoiding pesticides and chemical fertilizers. It was about being "natural," I thought, and somehow I translated that into meaning I should not add anything to the soil. My plants were getting air, water, and sunlight—that was enough. I mean, that's all they get "in the wild," right?

Wrong! Along with the fact that many of our annual food crops have been bred over centuries to become completely unnatural weaklings dependent on humans for their survival, our gardens do not function as natural ecosystems. Take a forest, for example. It feeds itself: leaves, branches, and eventually whole trees fall to the ground to decompose, returning nutrients to the soil, and feeding the next generation of plants and trees. Animals provide nutrients with their poop, and when they die their bodies continue to feed the soil. That just doesn't happen in an urban garden, and, if it did, your neighbors would probably call the city to complain.

All this means we must step in and help provide some nutrients to our soil. The absolute best way to do this is to add compost. This bears repeating—if you add nothing else to your garden but your own homemade compost, your plants will be happy. Gardeners call this stuff "black gold" for good reason.

If compost is so great, why are a ton of fertilizers (organic and otherwise) sold at garden centers? Fertilizers are necessary in a couple of instances: when you run out of compost (there never seems to be enough) and when you are gardening in containers.

Although containers benefit from a light mulching of compost, they also need supplemental feeding. That's the nature of container gardening. Soil nutrients are constantly being taken up by the plants, which have less soil to draw from than they would if they were planted in the ground. And containers require more frequent watering, which leads to leaching and nutrient loss.

· ·

Opposite: Because container soil usually includes minimal nutrients, container-grown plants need fertilizing throughout the growing season.

Fertilizers

Synthetic fertilizers are out there to sway you with their promises of quick, lush growth, but don't be seduced! Your plants may see almost instant growth, but this often comes at a price. Unlike organic supplements such as compost or manure, synthetic fertilizers do nothing to improve the long-term structure and fertility of your soil. Plus, synthetic fertilizers are salt-based, and salts can build up in your soil and cause plants to become dehydrated. And that lush new growth? It can stress plants and attract pests. Better to stick with organic fertilizers, which release nutrients slowly and in lower doses.

Plants require many kinds of nutrients and minerals, but three main nutrients are vital and form the basis for most fertilizers: nitrogen, phosphorus, and potassium, or N-P-K. Whether organic or synthetic, fertilizers display the ratio of these three elements on the package. For example, a complete (all-purpose) organic fertilizer might read 4-4-4, which tells us that it contains 4 percent nitrogen, 4 percent phosphorus, and 4 percent potassium. A high nitrogen fertilizer such as blood meal might read 12-0-0, and a phosphorus-rich source such as bone meal might read 4-12-0. Although they may not be listed on the package, additional micronutrients are supplied by many organic fertilizers—score another point for the organic team.

If you know your soil has relatively balanced proportions of N, P, and K (for example, if you start with store-bought potting soil or you have the soil tested), a balanced, all-purpose fertilizer is a good bet. But if your soil lacks one or two of the major elements, or you want to apply a fertilizer for a specific purpose—say, to increase leafy green growth—you should know a little about what these elements do for your plants.

○ **N (Nitrogen).** Nitrogen promotes foliage growth. Nitrogen-rich fertilizers are a good choice for getting baby plants (seedlings that have developed at least a few leaves) off to a good start—but too much will create lots of lush growth at the expense of fruit production. Leafy vegetables such as lettuce, spinach, and kale can benefit from nitrogen fertilizers throughout the growing season. Too little nitrogen will result in yellowing leaves and stunted growth. Natural sources include blood meal, alfalfa meal, cottonseed meal, and liquid fish emulsion.

- **P (Phosphorus).** Phosphorous is required for root development, disease resistance, and fruit and flower production. Too little results in stunted growth and purplish leaves. All crops—but especially fruiting plants such as tomatoes and eggplants—benefit from fertilizers containing phosphorous. Applying a phosphorus-rich fertilizer just before a plant's fruiting stage will help to ensure good fruit development. Natural sources include bone meal, rock phosphate, and seabird and bat guano (poop).

- **K (Potassium).** Potassium, or potash, is essential for overall plant health and hardiness and is required throughout the growing season. Too little potassium results in poor yields and brown, curling leaves. Root crops respond well to potassium. Natural sources include greensand, kelp meal, and wood ash.

Above: Leafy greens such as Asian mesclun mix benefit from light feedings with a nitrogen-rich fertilizer.

Dynamic accumulators are plants that are especially adept at extracting nutrients from the soil through their root systems, which are often extensive. They store these nutrients in their leaves and tissues, which we can then use as a natural fertilizer. Most dynamic accumulators are considered weeds, which is awesome because they are abundant and often free for the taking.

One of the most common ways to use dynamic accumulators is to add their leaves to the compost pile—thus supercharging your compost. I like to grow comfrey next to my compost bin; its deep roots collect the nutrients from the compost filtering into the soil and it provides a super-convenient source of comfrey leaves for my compost.

Another popular use for dynamic accumulators is to make tea—not the kind you drink with biscuits, but the kind you feed your garden. Tea is easy to make—just stuff a container full of leaves, fill with water, and close the lid. Leave it to "brew" until it starts to stink (one or two weeks), and then apply it to the garden using a watering can or spray bottle.

You can also interplant dynamic accumulators with your crops to help improve nutrient availability in the soil. Be careful to choose only plants that will actually benefit your garden; some dynamic accumulators, such as horsetail, are invasive.

You can collect a few types from roadsides and ditches; others can be started from seed.

borage (*Borago officinalis*)
chamomile (*Matricaria recutita*)
chickweed (*Stellaria media*)
clovers (*Trifolium* spp.)
comfrey (*Symphytum officinale*)
dandelion (*Taraxacum officinale*)
dock (*Rumex obtusifolius*)
horsetail (*Equisetum* spp.)
kelp (various species)
lamb's quarters (*Chenopodium album*)
plantain (*Plantago* spp.)
salad burnet (*Sanguisorba minor*)
stinging nettle (*Urtica dioica*)
yarrow (*Achillea millefolium*)

Applying supplements

Organic matter such as compost, well-rotted manure, and leaf mold can be applied at any time; however, spring is considered ideal. Dig it into the soil before planting your seeds or transplants, add a handful to planting holes, or use it as a mulch during the growing season whenever your plants need a boost.

Granular (powdered) organic fertilizers such as blood meal, rock phosphate, greensand, or all-purpose mixes can also be dug in a few weeks prior to or during planting. You can also side dress (scratch a little into the soil around the base of a plant) during the growing season, but applying fertilizer near the roots is the ideal. Most granular organic fertilizers deliver nutrients slowly; their effects should last for a relatively long time, particularly with in-ground gardens.

Liquid fertilizers are useful, especially in container gardening, because they deliver nutrients efficiently and quickly. Liquid fish emulsion and liquid kelp are common liquid fertilizers, but you can also find fertilizers made from worm castings and other types of guano, and blood, feather, and bone meals. Most liquid fertilizers are mixed with water and applied once every two weeks during the growing season.

For all fertilizers, follow the instructions on the package carefully. Organic fertilizers are less likely to burn plants' roots because of the slow-release nature of organics; however, improper use of any fertilizer can harm plants.

Hopefully, you now have a greater appreciation for, and understanding of, the role that living soils play not only in producing healthy plants, but in feeding our planet. Think of yourself as the steward of your tiny plot of earth, and tend it wisely. Feed your soil, and it will feed you. Stepping off my soapbox, I'll move on to what you really came here to do: grow!

Right: Comfrey's deep roots mine nutrients from the soil and accumulate them in its leaves, which can then be cut back and used to improve the potency of your compost or brewed into a fertilizer tea.

Blood meal. Bone meal. Feather meal. Fish emulsion. A number of organic soil supplement ingredients sound pretty gruesome.

Fertilizers such as bone meal and blood meal are commonly recommended for organic gardeners. Although they are not synthetic products, these slaughterhouse byproducts are most likely not produced from organically raised animals. Even if you are not concerned about using non-organic animal products in your garden, let's face it—spray-dried blood is just icky.

Thankfully, vegan alternatives are available.

Instead of blood meal or fish emulsion, try alfalfa meal (look for products sourced from organically grown plants) or alfalfa pellets (sold as rabbit food) to raise your nitrogen levels. With an N-P-K ratio of about 3-1-2, alfalfa is a green manure that also provides a dose of phosphorus and potassium. Because it heats up in the soil (making it a great compost accelerator), do not add it to the planting hole or you might toast your plants.

Cottonseed meal, with a N-P-K ratio of approximately 7-2-2, is another good nitrogen source that is often available at feed stores. Cottonseed is acidic, however, so unless you intend to lower your soil's pH, avoid it or use in combination with lime.

Soft rock phosphate, with a N-P-K ratio of about 0-3-0, will raise your soil's phosphorous levels and is a good slow-release substitute for bone meal.

7

SOWING & GROWING

Time to get your hands dirty. Starting seeds is easy. You just push a seed into the dirt, right? Sure, the *how* is simple, but the *when* requires a bit more thought.

Plant a seed too early, and cold temperatures will prevent it from germinating. Plant it too late, and it won't have time to grow up and produce fruit before winter chills hit. Catching that planting window is the key to seed-starting success.

Of course, you don't have to start all your edibles from seed: buying ready-to-plant veggies from the nursery does have its merits. Whichever route you choose, this chapter will teach you how to get your garden started.

Opposite: Purple and sweet basil seedlings emerge from the soil. Start basil and other heat-loving edibles indoors to get a head start on the season; transplant them outside once the weather warms.

SOWING SEEDS

I never fail to be amazed by seeds—or the incredible bounty that I can harvest from what began as tiny, shriveled specks. Some beginning gardeners regard seed starting with a healthy dose of fear, but the fact is, seeds are designed to survive, thrive, and eventually reproduce. We simply help them along by providing a little loving care.

Where to sow

You can start seeds in two main ways: Start them indoors in little pots, to be transplanted outdoors once the time is right. Or plant them outdoors in the place you want them to grow and mature into their full-grown selves.

If planting them directly outdoors sounds easier, it is—at least for you. Starting seeds indoors can be more involved. But some vegetables, especially warm-season crops such as tomatoes, melons, eggplant, and peppers, need to be started indoors, because they require consistent warmth and a long growing season. In most climates (I'm not talking about you, California), by the time the soil is warm enough for their seeds to germinate outdoors, these plants won't have time to produce a crop before chilly autumn temperatures roll around again. So we start them indoors, weeks before the last frost date, and then transplant them outdoors after temperatures warm up. Not all seeds can or should be started indoors, however. Some plants, notably root crops such as carrots and beets, do not like to be disturbed once they have, well, put down roots.

If you'd rather not start your own seeds, you can buy vegetable seedlings, also known as starts or transplants, from a nursery. But many gardeners start their plants from seeds for a couple good reasons. First, seeds are almost always cheap, and sometimes free. You can get 500 lettuce seeds for the same price as a six-pack of lettuce transplants. Second, finding seeds for the more uncommon types of vegetables is easier than finding transplants (think purple carrots and wrinkled heirloom tomatoes).

WHERE TO GET SEEDS

You can acquire seeds from many sources, including the rack at the garden center. I do most of my seed shopping online. For some reason, this allows me to think more clearly and not be swayed by the pretty packets at the checkout. Online shopping also offers more diversity; these suppliers often sell heirloom and specialty seeds. You can purchase the exact type of tomato you want, rather than settle for what is available at the garden store.

Seed-swapping events are great opportunities to share surpluses with other gardeners and, of course, to get seeds. Many botanical and community gardens facilitate these events. Seed swapping also happens online (search "swap seeds").

If you find yourself standing in front of the seed racks at the garden center, look for a few things on the packet before you buy. Try to purchase seeds from a reputable local seed company. These seeds will have been produced in a climate similar or equal to yours, so the seeds will produce plants that have adapted to your growing area. Also look at the sell-by date on the packet; make sure the seeds are intended for the current year. If you can find organic seeds, choose them, because they will have already adapted to organic growing conditions. Finally, if you want to save the seeds your plants produce at the end of the season, look for seeds marked "OP" (open-pollinated).

Opposite, clockwise from top left: Seed packets often contain more seeds that you can use in a small garden, so to avoid wasting unused seeds, coordinate your purchases with fellow gardeners and share them among friends. // Larger seeds, such as beans, are easy to handle and plant. // Planting seed is a great project for kids. // Choose quick-germinating veggies such as corn, cucumbers, lettuce, or radishes to hold their interest. Starting seeds indoors in containers gives you a jump on the planting season.

Seed needs

Seeds require moisture, warmth, light, and oxygen to germinate. But like most things in gardening, it all starts with the soil.

○ **Soil.** Seeds prefer a light, airy medium that provides good air circulation and allows for effortless root development; it should hold moisture but should not get soggy.

If you are planting directly outdoors, give your planting bed a once-over with a cultivator to provide the loose, fine soil seeds require. This is also a good opportunity to amend your soil with compost.

If you're starting seeds indoors, use a seed-starting mix, a light and fluffy, sterile blend of peat or coir, perlite, and vermiculite (or make your own using an equal blend of the three). A sterile mix is considered ideal, because garden soil and compost contain living organisms that can introduce diseases. They might also contain weed seeds.

○ **Containers.** You can start seeds in pretty much anything, from recycled yogurt containers to store-bought plastic cell packs. Plastic pots work fine for seed starting. Forget those cute little terracotta pots at the nursery—they allow the soil to dry out too quickly, and ditto for compressed peat pellets.

Newspaper pots are great for plants that don't like to have their roots disturbed, since you can plant the entire pot. And you can make them yourself. You can find instructions online (search "newspaper seedling pots") and make a free supply of seed-starting pots in no time. Don't use them for seeds that require a long period of time indoors before planting out, because the newspaper may break down before plants are ready to transplant. Plantable pots made of newspaper, coir, or other biodegradable material must be thin enough (and must break down fast enough) for plants' roots to be able to penetrate the walls with little effort.

Choose containers that will allow your seedlings room to develop, or be prepared to move plants into larger homes if they outgrow their pots before they are ready to go outside.

○ **Moisture.** Maintaining consistent moisture is crucial to success in seed starting. Your aim is to keep the soil consistently sponge-damp; fluctuating

Opposite: Newspaper pots make great seed-starting containers, because you can plant the pot with the plant.

Below: When it comes to seed starting, fluorescent lighting is a great indoor substitute for sunlight.

from bone-dry to sopping wet is torture to sensitive seedlings. Use a watering can with a fine rose nozzle, a spray bottle, or, even better, water from below. Place your pots in a tray or sink filled with 1 in. (2.5 cm) of water and let them soak it up. Don't let them sit in the water for too long—half an hour should do the trick.

○ **Warmth.** Some seeds, such as peas and other early-season vegetables, prefer cool soil. Others, such as peppers and cucumbers, prefer a slightly balmier climate. Most seeds germinate best in temperatures from 60° to 75°F (16° to 24°C). But don't crank up the heat (and your gas bill), because there are better ways of providing warmth to germinating seeds.

Sit your seed trays on top of the fridge, on a sunny window ledge, or on a warm oven. You can move the trays after the seeds have germinated—although some plants, such as peppers, prefer extra warmth even after they have sprouted.

It may be worth investing in a special heating mat that provides warmth from the bottom (which seeds love), or rigging up your own bottom-heat source. Some people position a 40-watt incandescent light bulb under a metal shelf or run outdoor Christmas-style rope lights through (clean) kitty litter, and then set their seed trays on top. My mom sets her trays on top of 1-gallon black plastic nursery pots with low-voltage shop lights inside. However you swing it, be careful not to start fires or electrocute yourself!

○ **Light.** After seedlings have emerged from the soil, they need a lot of light; without it, they grow leggy—tall, thin, and weak. Providing the light they want—14 to 16 hours a day—will probably be your biggest challenge in indoor growing.

A bright, sunny window will do, but this is not ideal (cloudy days combined with early spring's lack of daylight hours equal a light deficiency). If you want to get serious about seed starting, you can set up your own little grow operation using fluorescent lights. Believe it or not, you can use a couple of 40-watt fluorescent tube lights to keep your seedlings happy and healthy.

Hang the light from your ceiling, balance it on the backs of two chairs, mount it under a shelf—

however you do it, make sure you can either move the light or the plants up and down. Start out with the light about 3 to 4 in. (8 to 10 cm) above the seed trays and gradually increase the distance to about 4 to 6 in. (10 to 15 cm) as your plants grow.

Step-by-step: how to sow seeds

1. Moisten the soil before you sow. It should be damp but not wet—like a wrung-out sponge. This applies to outdoor (direct) sowing, too.

2. Fill your containers with soil mix. Tamp it down gently, leaving 1/2 in. (12 mm) or so of space at the top.

3. Check the seed packet for information on how deep to sow the seed. As a rule of thumb, seeds can be planted at a depth of about twice their diameter; thus large seeds such as beans will be sown deeper than miniscule carrot seeds. It is better to err on the side of planting too shallow, however; plant too deep and the seedling won't be able to reach the soil surface.

4. If you are sowing larger seeds in containers, poke a hole into the soil using a chopstick or pencil, place one seed in, and cover it with soil. For smaller seeds, sprinkle them on top and scratch them in. Depending on the size of your container, you might plant two to six seeds. Planting extra provides a fallback in case one or more fails to germinate. If you are sowing outdoors, sow a row by creating a trench with the edge of your trowel, and then scatter or place seeds evenly along it. Follow the spacing directions on the seed packet. Of course, you don't have to plant in straight lines. Blocks or natural-looking drifts also work.

5. Label your containers or rows if you are sowing more than one type of seed.

6. Place the containers in a warm, bright area, and wait. (If you cover your trays with a clear dome or plastic bag, you may not even need to water again until the seeds germinate.) Some seeds germinate in days; others take weeks.

. . . .

Opposite: You'd go mad trying to sow individual tiny seeds, such as those of carrots and lettuce. Just sprinkle a pinch onto the surface and scratch them into the soil.

SEEDLING FEEDING AND THINNING

A plant's cotyledon, or seed, leaves are first to emerge from the soil. These leaves provide the growing plant with nutrition until its true leaves appear (the third and fourth leaves to develop) and it's time to fertilize. Sterile seed-starting mixes provide no nutrients, so after true leaves appear, feed your seedlings weekly (and weakly) with a liquid kelp/fish emulsion combo (or add kelp one week and fish the next). If you added a little compost or worm castings to your seed-starting mix, you can skip this step.

At this stage, you need to make tough decisions about what to do with all those little seedlings that have germinated. Seedlings need breathing room for both roots and shoots, and keeping them tightly packed together means none of them will thrive. So you must thin them out, cutting off the weakest at soil level. Aim to leave only one seedling per 3 in. (8 cm) pot; in larger pots you can leave two. Thinning does not have to be a total waste of little plants: most seedlings are delicious in a salad.

In outdoor gardens, thin seedlings in stages; if you thin to the final spacing distance too early, you may wind up with fewer plants than you intended, since bugs and slugs can make suppers out of the remaining tender seedlings.

HARDENING OFF

Your indoor seedlings have had a pretty sheltered upbringing. To put them directly outdoors without preparation would be like us getting dropped in Antarctica without a jacket. Seedlings started indoors need to go through a toughening-up regime called hardening off before being planted outside.

Hardening off involves setting your pots of seedlings outdoors for increasingly longer periods of time to get them accustomed to the elements. Start by setting them in the shade—direct sun would be more than they could take—for about an hour. During the next several days, repeat this little field trip, slowly lengthening their outdoor visits, but bringing them back indoors for the night. You will also start introducing them to sun, and eventually (after a week or so), you can leave them out overnight.

Feel free to skip a day if the weather is particularly brutal. Cold frames, like mini greenhouses, allow you to skip all this schlepping inside and out. Just plunk your plants into the cold frame for two weeks, opening the lid for longer and longer periods of time each day.

TRANSPLANTING

After seedlings have been hardened off, they are ready for more permanent digs. Whether you are planting them in the ground or in a larger container, it's great to see your babies planted in their forever homes (even if you do end up eating them after a few weeks).

To start, dig the planting hole slightly deeper and about twice as wide as the plant pot. Unless you have already amended your soil with compost or a complete organic fertilizer, do this now, before adding the plant.

Squeeze the sides of your pot to release the plant. You may need to tap the rim gently. Try not to handle the seedling. If you must, hold it by its leaves—ideally, by its seed leaves, if it still has them—never by the stem.

Place the seedling in its hole, making sure its soil is level with the surrounding soil. Do not bury the stem, except in certain cases, such as tomatoes, which benefit from being planted deeply. Gently fill in the remainder of the hole with soil, and water well. That's it!

. . . .

Opposite, top: Remove overcrowded seedlings as they grow, eventually thinning to the spacing distance recommended on the seed packet.

Opposite, bottom, left to right: Test the size of the planting hole prior to removing the plant from its pot. // Never pull the plant out of its pot by its stem or leaves; instead, squeeze the sides of the pot to release the roots and let it slide out. // Gently lower the transplant into the hole; it should sit at the same soil level it was in its pot.

Planting Trees

Fruit trees are often sold as bare-root stock, which is exactly what it sounds like: the roots are bare, with no soil around them. Understandably, bare-root stock is sold in the winter months when the trees are dormant.

If you purchase bare-root stock, soak the roots overnight prior to planting. Dig a hole (or choose a container) approximately twice the diameter of the tree's root system, and loosen the soil on the walls of the hole to make it easier for the roots to spread. Next, put some soil back into the hole, mounting it up in the center. Spread the tree roots out over the mound. If you're planting a grafted tree such as a dwarfed apple, make sure that the graft union (the bulge where the rootstock meets the trunk) will be 2 to 3 in. (5 to 8 cm) above the soil line. Fill the hole with loose soil, pressing it down with your hands as you go. Water well. Many young fruit trees benefit from staking at the time of planting.

WHEN TO PLANT

A few factors determine the best time to sow or plant, including the plant's own nature. Is it a cool- or warm-season edible? Cool-season crops can handle lower temperatures and are usually planted in early spring or spring, or in late summer for an autumn, winter, or even spring harvest. In contrast, warm-season crops like the heat and are usually planted in late spring or early summer after the soil is nice and warm.

The average last frost date in your area is a huge factor in determining when to plant. Many seed packets say things such as, "direct sow at the time of last frost," or "start indoors 4–6 weeks prior to last frost." Go online to learn your area's average last frost date and to get a better idea of when your growing season starts.

After your seeds or starts are in the ground, the magic begins. But don't just sit back and watch the radishes grow—not yet, anyway. The next chapter tells you how to keep those precious little seedlings

. . . .

Opposite: Cool season root crops, such as beets, prefer to be direct sown in spring while the weather is cool.

KEEPING PLANTS HEALTHY

After you have sown your seeds and planted your crops, you can move into defense mode. Your newly planted seedlings are like candy to all sorts of insects, and a weed needs no better invitation than a freshly tilled bed. But although weeds, pests, and diseases are all part of gardening, you don't have to resign yourself to losing half your crop or using chemicals to combat them. There are better ways to deal with problems and maintain a garden.

Repeat this mantra: healthy gardens start with healthy soil. If your soil is healthy, your plants will be healthy. And healthy plants are better able to withstand pests and disease. This is one of the most important lessons of organic gardening, so learn it and put it into practice.

Opposite, top: Try to keep a sense of humor about garden pests and accept the fact that you might end up sharing some of your harvest with them. *Opposite, bottom:* You can plant nectar-rich flowers and herbs to attract pollinators and other beneficial insects to your garden. Photo by Andrea Bellamy.

Soil management is just the beginning. Practicing good garden maintenance techniques will also go a long way toward growing thriving crops. Similarly, preventing pests and disease and knowing how to deal with emerging weeds are more effective than grappling with these problems after they have taken hold. In this chapter, you will learn how to prevent and treat the problems that inevitably spring up just as your seedlings start to poke up out of the ground.

GARDEN MAINTENANCE

Maintenance encompasses all the usual suspects: weeding, watering, pruning, and basic chores. These tasks can be highly enjoyable—or a huge pain—depending on your outlook, your tools, and your setup. Get the last two right, and your outlook might change dramatically.

Essential tools

At any garden center, you can be easily suckered in by the baffling array of tools and supplies and ornaments. But what do you actually need? One of the benefits of a small garden is that you don't need that much to take care of it. You don't need a wheelbarrow. You won't need power equipment. You may not even need a shovel.

For my money, a few tools are the bare essentials.

○ **Trowel** for preparing small planting holes for transplants and for scooping soil into containers. Basic.

○ **Hand cultivator or hoe** for loosening soil and preparing the ground for planting. These can be three-pronged forks, pared-down versions of the familiar long-handled hoe, or designs that combine the best of both.

○ **Stakes** for supporting vine tomatoes and climbers such as beans, peas, and squashes. Bamboo stakes are nice looking, while heavy-duty plastic is longer lasting; found twigs and branches are a funky budget option.

○ **Twine** for lashing stakes together into teepees. Yarn also works well.

○ **Watering can or hose** for watering, obviously. Make sure you get a variable-setting nozzle for your hose or a watering can with a rose (the attachment with tiny holes on the end of the spout). Self-coiling spiral hoses are a great small-space option.

• •

Left: A trowel is a garden essential.

Opposite, clockwise from top: Invest in a few sturdy tools that will last for years. // After you fill the reservoir in a self-watering container, the plant will have access to water for several days. // A watering can with a large rose is especially good for seedlings, because it lightly showers the plants, rather than overwhelming a small plant with a flood of water.

○ **Pruning shears** for cutting back branches and harvesting. Good-quality pruning shears (also known as pruners or secateurs) are a must if you plan to grow any sort of woody plant, such as a fruit tree or berry shrub. But they also come in handy for pruning vining tomato plants, harvesting thick-stemmed vegetables such as cabbages, or cutting woody herbs such as rosemary.

○ **Gloves** for protecting your hands. Gloves are not strictly necessary but are nice to have for mucky or prickly jobs—turning the compost or dealing with cucurbits. Many types of gloves are available, from breathable (but not prickle-proof) cloth to heavy-duty rubber or leather. The best combine fabric with rubber or leather, providing breathability and protection.

Above: Water that sits on a plant's leaves can invite disease. You can't do much about the rain, but you can avoid using overhead sprinklers or indiscriminate use of the spray nozzle.

WATERING

Because watering is pretty much a constant task, consider spending time and money to make it an easy one. I once abandoned a small container garden on my balcony because it had no nearby water access. After the warm weather hit, I had to lug watering can after watering can up a flight of stairs, sometimes twice a day. I am a dedicated gardener, but that was just nuts.

Don't set yourself up to fail: plan out your watering strategy in advance. Make sure a hose, tap, or water barrel is easy to access and close to the garden site. Get a large, lightweight watering can to reduce your trips to the tap (and strain on your back).

Even better, remove yourself from the picture; set up a drip or low-flow automatic watering system on a timer. This requires more work and cost at the beginning, but it will pay off when you want to go away on a summer weekend and none of your friends can come by and water your plants.

How to water

Three basic rules apply when it comes to watering.

1. **Water the soil, not the leaves.** Water that collects on a plant's leaves can promote disease, especially on leaves of nightshades (such as potatoes and tomatoes) and cucurbits (such as zucchini).

2. **Water in the morning.** Watering early in the morning allows plants to absorb water before the sun gets high and the air heats up, providing your plants with fuel to withstand the heat of the day. Watering in the morning also allows plenty of time for any water to evaporate from leaves, which reduces the possibility of fungal diseases encouraged by cooler nighttime temperatures. Second best is watering in the evening; least desirable is at midday.

3. **Water deeply, not more frequently.** Better to water infrequently for longer periods of time, allowing water to soak in thoroughly, than to lightly sprinkle the surface of the soil every day. Plants' roots go where the water is. If you water deeply, roots will grow deep into the soil, and the plants will be better able to withstand drought and winds. Shallow watering encourages root growth at the soil surface, leaving the plant without a strong anchor and with no defense against wind and drought.

How often you should water depends on a number of factors. Young seedlings and transplants require more frequent watering than do established plants and trees. All plants require more frequent watering in hot weather. Sandy soils do not hold water as well as clay soils that require less frequent watering. And, finally, container gardens need watering more often than in-ground gardens.

Several signs can indicate that a plant needs water, such as soil that is pulled away from the sides of a container, and plants with limp, floppy leaves. Before you let them get that far, try a variation on the cake-readiness test. Stick your finger into the soil past the first knuckle. If the soil feels dry and doesn't stick to your finger when you pull it out, add water. Small containers can be checked by lifting them up; you'll soon get a feel for how heavy they should be when well-watered.

LESS WATERING, MORE GARDENING

- **Water deeply.** In in-ground gardening situations, watering for a longer period of time once a week is better than a short sprinkle every day.

- **Add organic matter.** Amend your soil with compost, manure, or other organic matter, and it will hold water like a sponge. (Be careful not to add too much organic matter to container soil or it can become compacted.)

- **Mulch.** Layer on compost, pebbles, bark, leaf mold, straw, or newspaper, which will act like a blanket on the soil, reducing evaporation.

- **Use large containers.** The smaller the container, the more frequently you have to water. Remember that terracotta containers lose water quickly.

- **Use self-watering containers.** Self-watering containers have a reservoir in the bottom that you fill once a week or less, depending on the size of the reservoir. Most types of self-watering containers act by wicking water up through the potting mix, providing a steady source of water to plants. Ready-made self-watering containers are often pricey, but you can make your own. (Search online for "self-watering containers" for ideas and instructions.)

- **Use a soaker hose or drip irrigation.** Both options are great for slowly soaking the soil. A soaker hose is perforated with tiny holes all along its length; lay one in your garden bed and it will deliver water directly to each plant. Drip irrigation systems use a main hose to deliver water to multiple drippers or sprayers, which can be positioned at regular intervals or custom designed to reach each plant or container. These systems can stay in place year-round if properly winterized and can also be put on a timer for completely effortless watering.

STAKING AND TRELLISING

You could let your vegetable plants sprawl across the ground, but why? Staking them—training them or supporting them to grow upward—saves valuable garden space, prevents disease, and makes vegetables easier to harvest. Peas, pole beans, cucumbers, squash, melon, vining (indeterminate) tomatoes, kiwi, raspberries, blackberries, and grapes are all good candidates for vertical growing.

Install your trellis or stakes before or at planting time to avoid damaging roots later on. Train plants to climb by wrapping their tendrils around the stakes (in the case of peas and beans) or by tying their shoots to supports as they grow (cut up old pantyhose or soft rags to use as ties).

A teepee or obelisk can make a great garden focal point and can support a number of vertical growers such as peas, pole beans, and cucurbits. You can make your own out of bamboo stakes, sticks, metal poles, or lumber lashed together at the top.

A square or rectangular grid leaning against a wall can be used to support any climbing fruits and vegetables, especially heavier ones such as melons and squashes. Make your own out of wood, or look for old wrought iron gates or headboards.

Arbors and other overhead structures are perfect for supporting kiwis, grapes, and cucurbits. They can do double duty as shade-providers for you or for cool-season crops such as salad greens.

Tree stakes, which are thicker and taller than general-purpose garden stakes, can be used to support dwarf fruit trees and prevent them from breaking or leaning when weighed down with fruit.

Wires are great for keeping blackberries and raspberries contained. If berries are grown along a fence, their sprawling branches can be supported by running a wire along the length of the patch and securing both ends to the fence. In a free-standing patch, wooden posts with horizontal crossbars threaded with wire running on either side of the plants will corral them and keep them manageable. Clear fishing line is a good option if you would rather not see the supports; plastic-guarded clothesline wire also works well.

STAKING A FRUIT TREE

Many young fruit trees should be staked as they are planted; ask the nursery if this is the case when you purchase a tree. The most common method of staking is to use two tall stakes—one on either side of the tree—with the tree supported in the middle.

Drive the stakes into the ground in the undisturbed soil outside the planting hole. You can attach the tree to the stakes using wire or rope, and protect the tree from damage by wrapping the wire or rope in thick fabric or rubber (placing the wire or rope inside a piece of old garden hose works well). Place the supports as low as possible, and no more than two-thirds the height of the tree. Leave a little slack in the wire or rope so that the tree can move about in the wind slightly and thus develop a strong trunk and roots.

Opposite, top: An arbor provides support for a grapevine, which in turn provides a shady nook for a hammock. Photo by Andrea Bellamy.

Opposite, bottom left: An old iron gate mounted to a wall or fence makes a charming support for snap peas.

Opposite, bottom right: Provide climbing plants the support they need. They will be healthier and more productive, and you will have more room to grow.

PRUNING

Most annual vegetables require little if any pruning in the true sense of the word (indeterminate tomatoes are a notable exception). But even if you are not growing vines, shrubs, or trees, you should understand how pruning can help your plants. Pruning removes dead, dying, or diseased growth; improves air circulation; allows sunlight to reach and ripen fruits; and improves or controls the size and shape of a plant.

Pinching out

Pinching out—regularly removing the tips of a plant's new growth—causes the plant to produce side shoots, becoming bushier and more vigorous in the process. This old practice—which involves using your thumb and forefinger to prune soft growth—forces the plant to devote energy into producing new growth, increasing the harvest. Pinching out encourages a plant to develop multiple stems or flower heads; most vegetables do not need to be pruned in this way, but many herbs do.

Herbs, like all plants, want nothing more than to produce flowers and, thus, seed, continuing their genetic line. But for our (culinary) purposes, we want leaves, not flowers, so we pinch out the strongest new growth to prevent the plant from flowering. Many herbs benefit from being pinched back early and often, starting when young plants have produced four sets of true leaves.

Pruning tomatoes

Indeterminate, or vining, tomatoes should be pruned to keep them from becoming unwieldy beasts. Determinate, or bush, tomatoes do not need pruning; the seed packet or plant label should tell you which type you have. To prune indeterminate types, pinch out the shoots that develop between the main stem and its leaf branches. If these are left to grow, each of the shoots—called suckers—will develop into an offshoot the size of the main stem; the plant will produce more fruit if you remove these suckers. You can also remove any non-fruit–bearing stems and leaves (including flower trusses) at the end of summer to force the plant to put its energy into ripening existing fruits.

Pruning berry shrubs

Blueberry and cranberry bushes should be pruned in late winter or early spring, before new growth starts. Annual pruning encourages good fruit production. During the first year, strip off any flower buds to force the plant to put energy into root development. During the first two years, prune only the dead, damaged, and diseased branches. Starting in year three, prune out crossing branches and to allow light to penetrate into the center of the shrub. Prune back the tips of vigorous branches to encourage bushy growth. Starting in year five, cut back two of the oldest branches to the ground each year to encourage new growth. The best fruit is produced on two- and three-year-old branches.

Pruning cane fruits

Raspberries and blackberries can be pruned in autumn. Just remove all the canes that produced fruit that summer; cane fruits produce berries on year-old growth. You can also prune canes that have outgrown their space; cut them back to restrict their growth.

. . . .

Opposite: Prune a tree or plant to influence its shape and size.

Below, left to right: Suckers develop on tomato stems from the elbow between the main stem and leaf branch. // Pinch out suckers with your thumb and forefinger. // Your tomato will be more productive after the suckers are removed.

 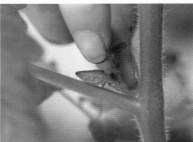 

Pruning fruit trees

Fruit trees are usually pruned to create good shape, and the shape that is right for your tree is usually determined by its type. Columnar trees, which grow to a maximum of 10 ft. (3 m) tall but only 2 ft. (60 cm) wide, are easily maintained by pruning side branches to the third leaf bud. Dwarf or semi-dwarf trees can be espaliered (trained to lie flat and often grown against a fence or wall) or pruned to create a vase-shaped open center, which allows sunlight and air to reach the center of the tree.

With all types of pruning, think about how you want the tree to look several years from now, and keep that in mind as you make your cuts. When removing limbs, make the cut parallel to the trunk and slightly in front of the limb's collar, which is the "wrinkled" area where the limb and tree trunk join together. When you prune branch tips, make diagonal cuts about 1/4 in. (6 mm) or so above a bud that faces out in the direction you want it to grow. Be careful not to prune out any fruiting spurs—short, gnarly branches that produce fruit. Pruning apples, pears, and other pome fruits is best done when the tree is dormant, in late winter or early spring before

trees begin to bud; however, if you want to reduce the overall size of the tree, prune in summer. Stone fruits such as apricots, cherries, and peaches should be pruned after flowering in spring.

To prune a tree into an open center shape, select four to six horizontal branches spaced evenly around the tree. They should be no more than 5 ft. (1.5 m) from the ground (lower is fine, too). These will form your vase shape and will serve as the main fruit producers. Next, cut back the main leader, or trunk, at an angle and just above the highest of your selected horizontal branches. This creates the open center. If your tree is young and does not have many horizontal branches, you can prune the trunk where you would like branches to grow (2 to 3 ft., or 60 to 90 cm, from the ground is suggested). New branches will grow just below this cut.

Fruit trees can also be espaliered, a method of pruning and training them into simple or elaborate patterns. Espaliered trees are especially popular for small gardens because they are trained flat and take up little space, yet they produce abundantly. Apples, apricots, figs, peaches, pears, plums, and nectarines are all good candidates for espalier.

The horizontal cordon is a popular and relatively easy espalier shape to create. An apple or pear tree in this shape can be grown along a wall or fence. (Once established, it can actually become a fence.) To train a tree into this shape, choose two lower branches as the lowest tier, or cordon. Loosely tie these branches to a horizontal support such as wires or a trellis, gradually tightening them over the following months until they are fully horizontal. Repeat with two or three sets of horizontal branches above this lowest cordon. Or, if the tree lacks suitable branches, cut the leader back to the lowest support. New growth will form at the pruning site, and you can begin to shape it to suit your will. After the tree has achieved the shape you want, regularly snip off errant growth to maintain the shape.

Left: The future shape of a tree depends on its early training. The first few years of growth and formative pruning are the most crucial. If you need help, contact an arborist or your local backyard orchard society.

Opposite: An apple tree grown as a horizontal cordon makes an attractive open fence.

WEEDS

One of the great things about having a small garden is that weeds are few. In containers, they may even be nonexistent. Weeds can be troublesome—even downright nasty—in an in-ground garden, however. Philosophical types might argue that a weed is just a plant in the wrong place, but weeds compete with crops for nutrients and space and can take over your garden if you fail to keep them at bay.

But they can also be helpful. Many weeds accumulate nutrients in their leaves, which can be harvested to add goodness to your compost. Others make a tasty addition to salads or sautés.

Without using chemical herbicides, you can control weeds in a number of ways using items you have around the house. Not all types of weeds will respond to one particular tactic; the best successes often result from a combination of methods.

Hand weeding

Hand weeding is a simple concept—yank out that plant—but not all weeds are so compliant. Many have deep taproots (such as dandelion) or extensive root systems (such as bindweed). These need to be dug out carefully, and you must make sure that you remove the entire root. Annual weeds are easily removed with a hoe or cultivator. Most weeds are easiest to remove when they are small and the soil is damp.

You can turn some weeds into food for the plants you do want in your garden by adding them to your compost. Compost only the leaves. Exclude flowers, seed heads, and the roots of perennial weeds or they will spread throughout your compost.

Mulching

Mulch is magic when it comes to weed control. Spreading organic mulch such as straw, leaf mold, or compost across the soil surface in a layer 2 to 4 in. (5 to 10 cm) thick will suppress weed growth, especially in combination with hand weeding. Do this regularly (at least twice a year), and you may never see weeds again. For really beastly weeds such as Japanese knotweed, a cover of thick plastic or old carpet is your best bet (cover this with mulch or build raised beds on top).

Sheet mulching is also a great way to create a new garden bed on top of soil that has been colonized by weeds. Smother the weeds with layers of cardboard, leaves, and manure, and let the worms turn it all into rich garden soil.

Other organic weed controls

If mulching and hand weeding are not working for you, you might consider a home-brewed herbicide. Many organic gardeners swear by a mixture of salt and vinegar—awesome on chips, deadly for weeds. Mix up a solution of 16 parts vinegar to 1 part salt, add a squirt of dish soap, and spray this onto weed leaves. It won't discriminate between crabgrass and collard greens—it will kill both—so apply it carefully. Avoid using it too close to vegetables, because the salts can disperse in the soil and can reach and kill the good plants. Salt and vinegar kill on contact, so the roots of the weed may survive and resprout. For perennial weeds, you may need to douse the plant with this solution to kill the roots.

Douse weeds that pop up between pavers and patio tiles with boiling water. Like vinegar, hot water is indiscriminate; avoid using this technique near plants you want to live.

ANNUAL VS. PERENNIAL WEEDS

An annual weed's entire mission is to produce a flower—and hence, seeds—in as little time as possible. Some can do this several times in one season, leaving their seeds in your soil so they can turn up to bug you next year. The trick with annual weeds is to remove them before they flower and set seed; pull them out as soon as you spot them. Common annual weeds include chickweed (*Stellaria media*), purple dead nettle (*Lamium purpureum*), groundsel (*Senecio vulgaris*), lamb's quarters or fat hen (*Chenopodium album*), common ragweed (*Ambrosia artemisiifolia*), hairy bittercress (*Cardamine hirsuta*), and speedwell (*Veronica arvensis*).

If annual weeds are a thorn in your side, perennials can be the bane of your existence. They come back year after year, sometimes despite repeated weeding and mulching. Tenacious perennial weeds such as bindweed (*Convolvulus spp.*) and Japanese knotweed (*Polygonum cuspidatum*) have extensive root systems and can regenerate from even a small piece of root left in the ground.

Remove perennial weeds as soon as you see them, and mulch regularly. Your aim is to prevent weeds from producing leaves; without leaves, the plant cannot produce energy and the roots will eventually die, although it can take several years in the case of persistent weeds. Common perennial weeds include dandelion (*Taraxacum officinale*), creeping buttercup (*Ranunculus repens*), horsetail (*Equisetum spp.*), bindweed (*Convolvulus spp.*), and stinging nettle (*Urtica dioica*).

Opposite, left: Planting in rows makes weeds easy to identify and remove..

Opposite, right: When the soil is damp, weeds are easier to remove.

PESTS

Unfortunately, you are not the only one looking forward to tasting your homegrown fruits and veggies. No matter where you live, pests seem to find your plants—even on a rooftop balcony. Having "bugs" mow down a fresh crop of veggies is infuriating, and it is natural to react by reaching for something entirely unnatural in defense. But pesticides really should not be your first line of attack.

Most chemical pesticides, whether slug bait or an insecticidal spray, are toxic not only to the pests they target, but also to curious children, pets, wildlife, and other innocent bystanders. Chemical pesticides also have a long-term detrimental effect on human and environmental health, which is why they are increasingly being banned from home use.

But even organic pesticides have their problems. They may be better for the environment, but they are still pesticides. Many are indiscriminate, killing the good bugs along with the bad. And although it might not seem like it, most insects are beneficial (or at least benign) in the garden. Although blasting those cursed aphids with home-brewed insecticidal soap might seem like a good idea, stop and look before you spray. Perhaps some lacewings are already on the case. It's just plain rude to kill insects that are helping you out.

It is a cliché, but when it comes to pest and disease control, the best offense truly is a good defense. Focus on maintaining healthy soil, rotating your crops, starting with clean pots and tools, and choosing disease-resistant edibles if you are concerned about pests or have experienced pest problems in the past. Finally, plant some good companions—let your plants do some of the work!

Right: Aphids cluster on a nasturtium, an edible flower commonly used as a trap crop for aphids. Aphids will flock to nasturtiums, which lure the pests away from other plants.

Opposite: Bees and other pollinators are hugely important forces in the garden.

SUPPORT WORKERS

Some insects and animals pollinate your crops and help control the population of destructive insects.

assassin bugs	hoverflies
bats	lacewings
big-eyed bugs	ladybugs
birds	mason bees
centipedes	minute pirate bugs
millipedes	praying mantids
damsel bugs	rove beetles
frogs and toads	soldier beetles
ground beetles	spiders
honeybees	wasps

Plant herbs and flowers to attract flying insects, provide perennial beds to protect existing populations, offer a water source, and layer on mulch to give crawling critters a place to hang out.

Companion planting

Companion planting is a classic organic gardening technique that involves matching plants that help each other in some way. You can choose plant companions that repel insects or attract pollinators, supply nitrogen, provide shade, or act as vertical support.

Some North American indigenous groups mastered this technique with the traditional "three sisters" grouping of corn, beans, and squash. Beans supply nitrogen to the corn and squash; corn stalks provide vertical support to climbing beans; and squash shades the soil, retaining moisture, while its prickly vines discourage squirrels and raccoons from accessing tender corn cobs.

The same genius can be applied in your garden. A smattering of well-chosen flowers throughout your veggie patch will attract pollinators and pest-eating insects, while others repel would-be snackers.

. . . .

Below: Marigolds, here interplanted with amaranth, are a classic choice for planting with edibles. Their distinctive scent is repellent to many pest insects.

Opposite: Borage is a large, pretty plant with delicate cucumber-flavored, edible flowers. It attracts predatory insects and honeybees.

Discouraging pests

Many strongly scented herbs and vegetables are supremely repellent to insect pests. Alliums—chives, garlic, shallots, onions, and leeks—repel slugs, snails, aphids, white flies, carrot rust flies, cabbage worms, and even some rodents. Plant them among carrots, brassicas, and pest-prone plants.

Many herbs and flowers do double duty as insect repellents. Basil, borage, dill, fennel, French marigold (*Tagetes patula*), mint, sage, and the inedible tansy (*Tanacetum vulgare*) look pretty and keep pests at bay.

Encouraging beneficial insects

Pollinators and other helpful insects can't resist anise hyssop (*Agastache foeniculum*), aster (*Aster* spp.), basil (*Ocimum basilicum*), bee balm (*Monarda didyma*), borage (*Borago officinalis*), calendula or pot marigold (*Calendula officinalis*), clover (*Trifolium* spp.), currant (*Ribes* spp.), dill (*Anethum graveolens*), lavender (*Lavandula angustifolia*), sweet alyssum (*Lobularia maritima*), yarrow (*Achillea millefolium*), and many other nectar- and pollen-rich flowers. Interplant these among your crops to attract bees, lacewings, ladybugs, and other beneficial bugs.

ORGANIC INSECT CONTROL

If your plants are suffering from a heavy pest infestation, an intervention might be required. Insects go after weak plants; sometimes the best thing to do is to remove and destroy the infested plant (tell yourself it's for the greater good).

The next least invasive approach is to trap or hand remove larger pests such as slugs and caterpillars, and use a strong jet of water to knock aphids and other soft-bodied insects off leaves. Repeat this on a daily basis, and you will soon see results.

If none of this is working and you are at your wits' end, you can consider a few products or techniques.

Sprays and powders.

Sprays and powders represent the strongest forms of organic pest control, but some are more benign than others. Although these products are not highly toxic to humans and other mammals, you should use caution when applying them. Wear a mask to avoid inhaling sprays or dusts, and wear a long-sleeved shirt and long pants to protect your skin.

○ **Biological control.** *Bacillus thuringiensis*, or Bt for short, is a naturally occurring bacterium that is sold to help control various insect pests. Applied

as a liquid spray or powder, Bt must be ingested by the insect to be effective. Several varieties of Bt selectively target specific pests, so be sure that you choose the one that will target the harmful bugs in your garden. Some Bt products kill caterpillars, and others target mosquitoes or Colorado potato beetles. Use Bt as a last resort; although it is far more selective than many insecticides, butterfly larvae are affected by its application. In addition, some insects are beginning to show resistance to Bt products.

○ **Homemade sprays.** You will find a million recipes for home-brewed insecticides and repellents floating around out there. The trouble with them—in addition to the fact that most do not discriminate between good and bad insects—is that they can harm your plants if they are improperly prepared or applied. The most common recipes call for various combinations of dish soap, garlic, citrus, or hot peppers. Feel free to experiment, but always test your sprays on a small area of your plant before going crazy with the spray bottle.

○ **Horticultural oils.** Oil sprays are primary used to control pests on fruit and nut trees and cane fruits. Often known as superior oils, these products work by smothering pests and their eggs. Superior oils are most commonly used when the tree or plant is dormant, but they can also be applied in summer when the plant is in full leaf. Spraying while the plant is dormant (generally in early spring as buds begin to swell but before any leaves emerge) can help prevent damage from overwintering insects. Follow package directions carefully.

○ **Insecticidal soap.** Insecticidal soap kills soft-bodied insects such as aphids, whiteflies, mites, and mealybugs on contact, which means you have to spray the actual insect, not merely the tops of the leaves. Insecticidal soap works by penetrating an insect's cuticle layer and killing it through dehydration. Although insecticidal soap is safe for the environment, it is also nonselective, which means it can kill beneficial insects, so be careful where you spray.

You can whip up your own insecticidal soap by mixing 1 tablespoon (15 ml) of biodegradable dish soap in 4 cups (1 L) of water. Never use antibacterial soaps, which can be harmful to plants. Look for a castile soap such as Dr. Bronner's. Test your homebrew on a small area of the plant, since homemade concoctions can vary in potency; you don't want to burn the plant's leaves. Insecticidal soaps are also available at garden centers and are specially formulated not to hurt your plants.

o **Neem.** Neem oil is derived from the seed of the neem tree, which has natural insecticidal properties. Spray it on your plants to repel or poison insects and prevent fungal growth. Neem is one of the few insecticides that is taken up by the plant, making the plant inedible—at least to insects. It will kill a range of pests including aphids, cabbage loopers, leaf miners, and whiteflies. Be sure to coat the entire surface of the plant.

Barriers and traps

Barriers and traps can also work effectively on some pests, and they are less disruptive than insecticides.

o **Fruit bags.** Protect apples and pears from codling moth damage by slipping paper bags over the developing fruit. Secure the bag in place with a twist tie or twine and remove it just before harvest.

o **Beer traps.** Slugs have a weakness for beer. Take advantage of this by luring them into a trap filled with brew. Bury a tuna can, aluminum pie plate, or other recycling bin find until the lip is level with the soil. Half fill it with beer. Slugs will climb in and drown—not a bad way to go, all things considered.

o **Copper.** Slugs and snails hate copper; it actually gives them an electric shock on contact. Protect plants from their damage by forming a copper ring around each plant individually or around the entire bed. You can acquire copper bands and tape for this purpose.

o **Diatomaceous earth and other abrasives.** Discourage slugs and snails, sowbugs, earwigs, and caterpillars by spreading a 2 in. (5 cm) wide barrier of diatomaceous earth, wood ash, sawdust, crushed eggshells, or seashells around your plants. These sharp-edged materials irritate the coatings of soft-bodied insects and cause them to dehydrate and die. These materials may need to be reapplied after rain.

o **Collars.** Protect seedlings from cutworms—caterpillars that live beneath the soil surface during the day and come out at night to feed on the stems of your seedlings—with a simple cardboard collar. Cut the tubes from toilet paper or paper towel rolls into 3 in. (8 cm) sections, place the tubes over the seedlings, and push them halfway into the soil.

o **Floating row covers.** A floating row cover is a sheet of fabric or plastic that you drape over your crops. They can be used in conjunction with hoop or other supports to hold the material off tender seedlings. Also used to extend the growing season (they protect plants from cool temperatures), floating row covers are effective for controlling many types of pests, including carrot rust flies, caterpillars, leafhoppers, and Colorado potato beetles.

Buy a commercial variety or make your own using mosquito netting or other sheer fabric. Drape the fabric over your beds or containers and weigh down the edges, letting out the fabric as the plants grow. Remove the covers after plants are sturdy enough to hold their own against pests, and remove them from cool-season crops after the weather gets warm. Some crops, such as cucurbits, need to be visited by pollinating insects to set fruit, so they should not be covered indefinitely. Carrots are an exception: keep them covered all season to protect them from the carrot rust fly, if these are a problem in your area.

o **Sticky traps.** The concept behind a sticky trap is simple: attract the pests to the trap through color or scent, and then trap them in a sticky coating. Dozens of these types of traps are available. Some are designed to target one specific pest, and others control a variety of flying insects and beetles. The simplest ones are bright yellow rectangular boards that you set near or above plants. Trunk bands, which wrap around the trunks of fruit trees, trap insects crawling up and down. Sticky traps are nonselective: they also trap beneficial insects.

o **Trap crops.** Sacrifice one for the good of many. That's the theory behind the trap crop. Trap crops are plants that attract insect pests away from your primary food crop. After the trap crop plant is infested with insects, it can be destroyed. Nasturtiums are commonly planted to attract aphids. Broad beans are also a good aphid trap crop. Mustard crops will attract cabbage worms, and chervil will attract slugs.

Predators, parasites, and nematodes

All garden pests have natural predators, and you can harness their hunger in your garden. After all, you planted all those beneficial insect-attracting plants just for this reason. But if the flowers and herbs are not doing their job and your plants are overrun with pests, get yourself some ladybugs or lacewings. These, and a host of other predatory and parasitic insects and nematodes, can be found online and at some garden centers. The type of predator you buy depends on what insects are eating your plants; make sure you buy the right one for the job. Ladybugs are voracious aphid eaters, for example, but they won't be able to help you with soil-dwelling grubs.

The great thing about this approach to pest control is that it can't hurt. If you release ladybugs and they fail to solve your aphid problem, you will be poorer, but that's about it. Your plants—and the environment—will not be harmed. On the downside, beneficial insects and nematodes can be expensive, and sometimes they fly away as soon as they are released. And don't think you can use insecticides—even organic ones—when these guys are working in your garden.

Common pests and how to beat them

Every year, it seems I encounter a new insect foe. Several of the most common garden pests, including some of my personal nemeses, are included here.

○ **Aphids.** These tiny, pear-shaped, soft-bodied insects can be green, gray, black, or pink. Aphids secrete sticky honeydew excrement that covers infested plants, attracting ants and black mold. Usually found in thick clusters, aphids suck the sap from plants, especially favoring tender new growth. Affected leaves and stems become twisted and weak. To control them, knock them off with a strong jet of water; attract or buy ladybugs, lacewings, or aphid midges; or spray with insecticidal soap or neem.

. . . .

Below, left: Ladybug larvae look like tiny, spiny alligators and have a voracious appetite for aphids. Photo by Andrea Bellamy.

Below, right: Ladybugs are an organic gardener's best friend. Photo by Andrea Bellamy.

- **Apple maggots.** White maggots that tunnel through apples, blueberries, and plums, apple maggots can be controlled by regularly collecting dropped fruit, hanging traps in trees during the growing season, bagging fruit, and attracting predatory ground beetles.

- **Cabbage maggots.** Adults look like common houseflies, but their larvae—small white maggots—do the damage, tunneling into the roots of brassicas and killing or stunting the plant. Use floating row covers to prevent adults from laying eggs or apply parasitic nematodes.

- **Carrot rust flies.** These shiny, small, black flies are attracted to young carrot plants, but they can also infest other umbellifers such as parsnips and celery. Their larvae do the damage; the little white maggots tunnel into roots, stunting or killing the plant. To control them, practice crop rotation; cover beds with floating row covers before seedlings emerge (and leave them covered until harvest); plant resistant cultivars, such as the 'Flyaway' carrot; and interplant your carrots with alliums.

- **Caterpillars.** Army worms, cabbage loopers, imported cabbage worms, cankerworms, leaf rollers, and tomato hornworms will eventually turn into harmless moths or butterflies, but in their larval (caterpillar) stage, they can destroy your garden—and your will to live. To control them, hand pick caterpillars daily, set sticky traps to catch adult moths, attract or release parasitic wasps, cover plants with floating row covers, and spray the plants with Bt as a last resort. Spray fruit trees with horticultural oil.

- **Codling moths.** The codling moth is a fruit tree pest that affects a range of stone and pome fruits, most commonly the apple. Its larvae tunnel into the fruit, spoiling them. To control them, spray the tree with horticultural oil, bag individual developing fruit, buy and release parasitic wasps to attack the eggs, and use sticky tree bands to trap the larvae as they climb up the trunk.

- **Colorado potato beetles.** The Colorado potato beetle and its larvae prey on plants in the nightshade family, feeding on the leaves. These yellow-and-black–striped beetles can be controlled by shaking them from plants (best done in the early morning when they are groggy). Place a cloth or newspaper under the plant for easy collection. You can also use mulch to attract ground beetle predators, spray infested plants with neem, and use floating row covers.

. . . .

Below: Leaf miners leave behind scribble-like tunnels on leafy greens. Photo by Andrea Bellamy.

o **Cucumber beetles.** Striped or spotted cucumber beetles feed on the leaves and roots of corn and squash plants, including, of course, cucumbers. To control them, shake them off the plants as you would Colorado potato beetles, attract or purchase parasitic nematodes, or use floating row covers (and hand-pollinate the flowers).

o **Cutworms.** Cutworm caterpillars emerge at night to feed on the stems of seedlings at the soil line, cutting stems in two. Control them using collars and attract predatory ground beetles by providing permanent plantings, mulch, and ground-covers (low-growing plants).

o **Flea beetles.** These tiny black or brown beetles get their name from their jumping habit, similar to that of fleas. They riddle the leaves of vegetable crops with little holes, sometimes killing seedlings. Use floating row covers, spray with neem, and create shady conditions (flea beetles are sun worshippers).

o **Leafhoppers.** These tiny, wedge-shaped insects spring like grasshoppers when disturbed. They suck sap from plants, causing leaves to curl and yellow. To control them, attract parasitic wasps or spray with insecticidal soap or neem.

o **Leaf miners.** You probably won't see these tiny black flies or their larvae, but you will see the damage in the form of pale "scribbles" on your leafy greens: the larvae leave this sign after tunneling through the leaf. Destroy these leaves. As a last resort, spray the plant with neem.

o **Mealybugs.** These small, oval, soft-bodied insects are covered in white, waxy fluff. Like aphids, they suck sap from plants, particularly new growth, and leave honeydew excrement behind. Knock them off with a strong jet of water, use mealybug destroyer larvae, or spray them with insecticidal soap.

o **Mexican bean beetles.** With their black spots, these pale orange, oval beetles look similar to ladybugs. They feed on plants from the legume family, skeletonizing the leaves. To control them, use floating row covers, release or attract predatory or parasitic insects, or spray with neem.

o **Mites.** Most of the many types of garden mites are nearly invisible to the naked eye. The most common garden pest is the spider mite, which sucks plant sap, weakening or in extreme cases killing the plant. Damage appears on the undersides of leaves as a speckling of light dots. If the mites are not controlled, leaves will turn yellow or bronze and fall off the plant. Fine webbing may be visible in heavy infestations. To control mites, attract beneficial insects such as lacewings and minute pirate bugs, spray the undersides of leaves with a strong jet of water, or spray the plant with insecticidal soap or neem. Spray fruit trees with horticultural oil.

o **Nematodes.** Some types of nematodes are helpful and are sold to control pest insects. Other nematodes are harmful plant parasites, causing damage to roots, stems, and leaves. If you think pest nematodes have taken up residence in your soil, practice crop rotation, and plant a cover crop of marigolds, which suppresses the microscopic worms.

o **Plum curculios.** These warty-looking beetles lay eggs inside the fruits of apple, apricot, cherry, peach, and of course, plum trees. Infested fruit, which usually drops prematurely, shows a crescent moon–shaped scar in the flesh where the eggs were deposited. To control them, spread a sheet beneath the tree and shake or jar the pests onto the sheet; collect and destroy them.

o **Slugs and snails.** Slugs and snails love to munch on seedlings and leaves, leaving their distinguishing trail of slime as they go. Set up barriers such as copper strips or abrasives, set out beer traps, hand pick the critters on rainy days or in the early morning when they are out and about, and encourage predatory ground beetles.

o **Squash vine borers.** Narrow red and brown moths produce larvae that bore into the vines of squash plants, causing vines to wilt or die. To control them, use floating row covers (do the pollinating yourself or remove the covers later in the season).

o **Whiteflies.** Tiny whiteflies congregate on the undersides of leaves, sucking plant sap and weakening plants. Like aphids and mealybugs, they secrete honeydew, which promotes the growth of mold. Use sticky traps, attract predators and parasites such as ground beetles and wasps, and spray them with insecticidal soap or neem.

o **Wireworms.** Wireworms are the larvae of the click beetle, which, when turned on its back, produces an audible click as it rights itself. Grains, carrots, and potatoes are favorites of the wire-worm, which bores into roots or tubers. Garden beds that replace lawn are particularly susceptible, since wireworms hang out in sod. To control them, cultivate the soil deeply to destroy larvae or apply parasitic nematodes.

Other Pests

Insects are not the only pests that can dampen your gardening spirits. Even if you haven't met them yet, you are sure to meet your local wildlife if you grow food.

○ **Small mammals such as squirrels, rats, and raccoons** love to get their paws on fresh produce. Grow squash and prickly berries as a barrier around corn, tomatoes, and other favorites, or erect a chicken wire cage around your containers. Lining the inside of raised beds with hardware cloth can control the damage caused by gophers and other tunneling mammals.

○ **Cats and dogs** can also be pests. Cats love to use cultivated soil as a litter box. To prevent this, cover freshly seeded beds with chicken wire until plants are larger, or invest in an electronic device that frightens cats and dogs away with sound or a water spray. Dogs can trample and pee on plants, but usually even a low fence will keep them off your edibles.

○ **Birds** are wonderful to have in your garden, until they start eating your ripening fruit or grains. The most surefire way to protect your plants is by covering them with netting or cages, but you can also try scaring birds off by hanging reflectors, noisemakers, or whirligigs, or by setting out plastic snakes. Switch up your tactics to keep them working effectively.

○ **Humans** also cause their share of damage in the garden. Many people have no qualms about stealing your ripe tomatoes or cucumbers or walking through your beds. A low fence can help reinforce boundaries; also try planting easy-to-steal edibles at the back of the bed. Children, especially toddlers, can also be a force of destruction. My daughter loves to pluck unripe tomatoes, upend containers, and throw handfuls of dirt. Other than developing a level of tolerance for chaos, my strategy is to distract her with her own container full of dirt and a shovel, and I do larger garden tasks during her nap time.

Below: Gardening with a small child? Cultivate tolerance for chaos and half-finished tasks. Photo by Ben Garfinkel.

DISEASES

If it's not mites, it's mildew. Fortunately, many common plant diseases are relatively easy to prevent, or at least control, using good cultural practices. Crop rotation, cleaning up leaf and plant debris, destroying (not composting) diseased plant matter, watering effectively, choosing disease-resistant plants, fertilizing properly, and pruning to promote good health all go a long way in preventing the spread of disease. That said, sometimes despite all your best efforts, disease is inevitable.

Weeds, disease, and pests can get you down. I have battled my share, and I understand the frustration they cause. I guess the upside is that we can learn from our gardens and make improvements as we go. Every year that I garden, I gain a deeper understanding of the necessity of prevention and of good garden maintenance, of companion planting, and of continuing to build healthy soil. The pests or diseases that do come along point out where I am falling short. So try your best at prevention, and deal with the inevitable pests as they arise. Learn your weaknesses, and make changes next year. Refine. Integrate. And move on.

○ **Bacterial canker.** Bacterial canker affects fruits such as apricot, cherry, peach, and plum, causing branches to wilt and die. Oozing lesions on the branches emit a red, sour-smelling gum. Prune off infected branches, sterilizing pruning shears between cuts with a quick dip in a 1:2 hydrogen peroxide and water bath to prevent the spread of the disease.

○ **Blight.** Tomatoes, potatoes, and other nightshades are susceptible both to early and late blight, fungal diseases that cause dark spots on leaves and eventually stems. Both types can overwinter in the soil, and this is why you should avoid planting nightshades in the same place year after year. Late blight thrives in cool, damp weather; prevent it by avoiding overhead watering (move or plant tomatoes under cover to avoid direct rainfall). Destroy infected plants, and do not compost them.

○ **Blossom end rot.** If a tomato or pepper fruit has a dark, rotten-looking spot on the bottom, the plant has been infected with blossom end rot. It is the result of a calcium deficiency, often caused by erratic watering. Keeping the soil evenly moist can prevent rot from affecting the next crop.

○ **Brown rot.** Apricots, cherries, peaches, and plums are susceptible to brown rot, especially in humid areas. This fungal disease causes brown spots to form on fruits, eventually destroying them. It can also cause blossoms to die. To control it, remove and destroy damaged fruit and any branches showing lesions. Sulfur or copper sprays also help.

○ **Clubroot.** This fungal infection attacks the roots of brassicas. It causes roots to swell and become twisted, preventing them from absorbing water. Affected plants appear stunted or wilted. Unfortunately, clubroot lingers in the soil; do not replant brassicas in an infected spot for several years. You can control clubroot by adding lime to raise the soil pH to at least 7.2, because the fungus prefers acidic soils.

○ **Damping-off.** Damping-off fungi attack newborn seedlings, causing them to keel over at soil level. The lower stems of affected seedlings usually appear thin and dark, as if crushed or rotting. Damping-off also affects seeds before they sprout. Good hygiene will prevent damping-off. Start seeds in sterilized containers and soil, provide excellent drainage and air circulation, and do not overwater.

○ **Fire blight.** This bacterial disease affects apple and pear trees. It causes leaves to blacken and growing tips to curl; if you do nothing to control fire blight, it can kill the entire tree. Prune off affected branches well below the infected areas, sterilizing pruning shears between cuts. In winter, inspect branches for cankers and prune them out.

○ **Mildews.** Downy and powdery mildews are fungal diseases that affect leaves and sometimes fruit. Downy mildew, which appears as yellow or brown spots on the tops of leaves and downy spots on the bottoms, is most prevalent in cool, damp weather. To control, avoid overhead watering and spray with neem. Powdery mildew looks like a dusting of flour across the leaf surface. Squash plants are particularly susceptible. Unlike downy mildew, powdery mildew thrives in hot, humid weather and in shade. Prune out infected leaves to promote good airflow; move plants to a sunnier locale, or spray with neem.

- **Mosaic viruses.** Mainly affecting cucurbits such as cucumbers and squash, mosaic viruses cause yellow or white patches to appear on foliage, sometimes causing fruit to become misshapen. Destroy infected plants. Control aphids and cucumber beetles, which spread the disease.

- **Peach leaf curl.** A virus affecting peaches and nectarines, peach leaf curl causes leaves to become distorted and reddish. Infected leaves drop early, and fruit production is reduced. Choose resistant cultivars, or control the disease using lime sulfur sprays.

- **Rust.** This fungal disease appears in the form of rust-colored spots or streaks on leaves. To control, remove and destroy infected parts; dust with sulfur to control mild cases, and practice crop rotation.

- **Scab.** Various types of scab commonly affect potatoes and other root crops, as well as apples and other fruit trees. Scab is a fungal infection that causes brown or dark green rough spots on fruit or roots. Prevent potato scab by practicing crop rotation and planting resistant selections. In fruit trees, prevent infection by cleaning up leaves and dropped fruit each fall, and spray trees with copper or sulfur. Prune to promote good air circulation, and choose resistant plants.

- **Wilt.** Fusarium wilt and verticillium wilt cause plants to, well, wilt. Leaves turn yellow and drop, and plants may die. These fungi affect a range of plants and remain in the soil for years, making crop rotation ineffective. Fusarium wilt is common in warm temperatures, and verticillium wilt favors cool climates. Choose resistant plants, and remove and destroy infected plants.

. . . .

Below, left: Powdery mildew, which commonly plagues cucurbits, can be controlled by pruning out infected leaves.

Below, right: Blossom end rot on a tomato is caused by fluctuating soil moisture (from inconsistent watering) and low levels of calcium in the soil.

Opposite: Like other alliums, garlic is susceptible to rust—especially in wet conditions. If left unchecked, rust can result in diminished bulb size..

MAKING THE MOST OF LIMITED SPACE

When you want to grow a lot of food in a small space, every square inch of soil has to work extra hard. Experienced small-space gardeners use a number of techniques to get the most from their gardens. Practicing succession planting, vertical growing, and winter gardening, for example, can make a big difference because these techniques allow you to harvest more food over a longer season. Learn the basics, and then put them into practice in your garden.

Opposite: This two-tiered planter makes clever use of space and maximizes available light.

SUCCESSION PLANTING

Succession planting is a technique that will let you harvest a succession of crops from a single plot or container. For example, you might start off early in the spring with a sowing of arugula or radishes—cold-tolerant crops that mature quickly. You could then follow these early crops with main-season edibles such as beans, cucumbers, or tomatoes; then, in late summer as these are being harvested, you could plant another cool-season crop such as endive or kale for fall or winter harvest.

The idea is not to let valuable garden space sit idle, and to be ready to plant something new whenever a space opens up. In fact, you often need not harvest the last crop before planting the next; you can interplant your new crop while the last crop is still in the ground. Just time it so that when the new crop starts to need more space, the old crop will be ready to harvest and clear out. You can also sow seeds at the same time you plant seedlings of the same type; the transplants will give you a jump on the next harvest.

The term *succession planting* is also used to describe planting the same edible in one- to three-week intervals, depending on how long it takes the particular type of vegetable to reach maturity. With this type of planting, also known as succession sowing, you can extend the period of harvest and avoid a glut of one particular crop. Crops that mature quickly are great candidates: consider arugula, beans, beets, carrots, lettuce and salad greens, radishes, scallions, and spinach.

INTERPLANTING

You can maximize your yields by taking advantage of plants that grow at different rates or at different root depths and planting them together. For example, you can plant quick-growing lettuces alongside your tomato seedlings; you will have harvested several salads' worth before your tomatoes even start to ripen. As your tomatoes grow, they will provide a bit of shade to keep your greens from bolting in the heat. Many companion planting principles can be applied to interplanting techniques; combine the two for truly awesome results.

Right: Romaine lettuce takes up little space when grown on decorative metal shelving.

CUT-AND-COME-AGAIN CROPS

When harvesting looseleaf lettuces and other greens, rather than pulling out the entire plant, just remove a few of the outer leaves for your salad or meal; the plant will continue to produce new leaves. Some types of greens, notably mesclun (a mix of various greens and lettuces), can be cut off right at the stem when they are young seedlings. They will regrow, and you can repeat the process two or three times throughout the season. Arugula, Chinese cabbage, chard, chervil, chicory, collard greens, cress, dandelion, endive, escarole, kale, leaf lettuces, mizuna, and mustard are good cut-and-come-again candidates.

VERTICAL GARDENING

Grow anything you can up stakes, teepees, trellises, or arbors—not only will vertical gardening make the most of valuable garden space, but it also packs a great visual punch. Think of trellises or screens as the living walls in your garden house—decorate with green! The usual suspects include peas, pole beans, tomatoes, berries, kiwis, and grapes, but cucumbers, squash, and melons can also be trained upward on sturdy supports.

. . . .

Below: Blackberries, raspberries, currants, and other climbing berries can be grown against a fence or wall.

STRETCHING THE GROWING SEASON

Season-extension techniques allow you to grow food beyond the main gardening season. Start by introducing yourself to cool-season crops—plants that enjoy cooler spring or fall temperatures. If you limit yourself to tomatoes and cucumbers, your garden won't see any action until late spring or early summer. Cool-season crops such as lettuces and peas can go into the ground long before that. But you can use a few tricks to get your crops growing even earlier in the spring, or to hold in the garden well into the fall or winter, and they all act by keeping the soil warm using cloches, cold frames, row covers, and plastic mulches.

Cloches

Cloches are open-bottomed protective coverings that can be placed over tender seedlings to protect them from frost and wind-chill. Traditional cloches were bell-shaped (*cloche* is French for bell) and made of glass. Cloches can be made of glass, plastic, terracotta, or even bamboo. Cloches are great for protecting tender plants against unexpected early spring frosts or for easing seedlings out into the world during their hardening-off period. You can easily make yourself a whole supply of not-so-pretty cloches by cutting the bottoms off plastic jugs or bottles. Place a bottomless bottle over a seedling and gently push it into the soil to secure it. Just make sure to remove the cloches on hot, sunny days or you risk frying your seedlings.

Cold frames

A cold frame works on the same principle as a cloche—it protects plants by acting as a mini greenhouse—but with room for multiple plants. These simple contraptions allow you to harvest many cool-season crops year-round, even in areas with cold winters. Cold frames can also give you a jump on spring by providing a sheltered place where sowed seeds can sprout and grow. (You can transplant them to the garden after the weather warms.) They can also be used as transitional housing for seedlings during their hardening-off stage.

A cold frame has two essential parts: a base, which is a frame made of plywood, reclaimed brick, old pallets, cinderblock, or even bales of hay; and a lid created from an old window, a sheet of rigid acrylic material, or thick plastic sheeting.

You can buy ready-made cold frames, but you should be able to make your own quite easily—and for almost free—using salvaged materials. Construct the base in a four-sided, rectangular shape, positioning it where it will receive sun for most of the day. The back of the base of most cold frames is slightly higher than the front; this allows for maximum sun exposure and heat capture. The walls of the base should be draft-resistant to provide good insulation for tender plants. The lid can be simply laid on top, perhaps adding some weather stripping around the edges to prevent drafts, or it can be attached with hinges. As with cloches, the lid should be propped open or removed on hot days so that your plants avoid overheating.

Row covers

Floating row covers, also used to protect plants from certain types of insect pests, can make great season-extension tools. Lightweight fabrics can be laid directly over your plants or propped up with stakes or hoops. The edges can be secured with stones, handfuls of soil, or a length of wood. Like cloches and cold frames, row covers create a micro-climate for the enclosed crops, raising the ambient temperature. Row covers are especially good for protecting late-summer and fall crops against early frosts. Row cover fabric is available in several different weights; look for the type that offers frost protection.

Plastic mulches

Spreading plastic mulches over prepared soil will allow you to plant warm-season crops such as peppers, melons, and cucumbers earlier in the season; the soil warms after the mulch absorbs heat from the sun. Black plastic is the most common type, which is also used for weed control and to reduce evaporation. You can also find silver, red, or green plastic mulches, each created for specific purposes or types of crops, as well as biodegradable mulches. Cover the soil a week or more before you intend to plant, burying the edges into the soil. Cut an X in the plastic wherever you want to plant, and then tuck in seeds or transplants.

Opposite, left: A classic bell-shaped glass cloche protects a young basil seedling from frost.

Opposite, right: A cold frame provides shelter from early spring frosts; an old skylight window serves as a lid.

WINTER GARDENING

The ultimate in succession planting, winter gardening is all about maximizing your space and your harvest. The phrase *winter gardening* is a bit of a misnomer—at least for those of us who cannot do any planting or active gardening during the cold winter months. It is completely possible, however, to harvest food from your garden throughout the winter and early spring.

The key to winter gardening is summer through late-summer planting for most vegetables. Do not plant spinach in late autumn and expect a winter harvest—it just won't happen. A winter garden is like a refrigerator: food stays fresh and ready to eat, but it does not put on any growth. Day length is the critical factor. As the days get shorter, growth slows. By late fall/early winter, plants are pretty much in hibernation mode until the days start to lengthen again in early spring. The goal is to have your plants reach their full size by Halloween, ready for eating throughout the winter. Don't automatically pull them out if they are not ready, though. You can leave cold-tolerant veggies in the ground; they might surprise you by throwing out some new growth when the days start to lengthen.

It's difficult to imagine planting your winter garden in the heat of summer, and often you won't have the room to plant anything until your warm-season edibles have vacated their beds or containers. One way around this is to start your winter-garden seeds in flats and transplant them into their final homes after the tomatoes and zucchini have been cleared out.

In mild climates, many veggies may happily hang out without protection from the cold (although mulch and protection from wind and excess rain never hurts). In colder climates, cold frames may be necessary to ensure a winter harvest.

Cool-season and winter garden vegetables

Cool-season annual crops are the first to go in the ground in spring, and they are often the last to be planted in summer or fall for a winter harvest. Many quick-maturing types can bookend your warm (main) season crops to get the maximum use out of a particular bed, and most make good candidates for the winter garden.

Many edibles actually taste better after a frost. They produce a natural antifreeze—sugar—that translates into a sweeter-tasting vegetable. Just one more reason to stretch your growing season.

Some of these techniques may take a little more planning and effort, but the result—a more productive and efficient garden—is totally worth the effort, especially if you are keen to maximize your harvests.

Opposite: Kale is an attractive and hardy leafy green that can be harvested throughout the winter in many climates. Photo by Andrea Bellamy.

EDIBLES FOR THE WINTER GARDEN

VEGETABLES	HARDINESS
arugula (rocket)	HH
beets	HH
bok choy	HH
broad beans	H
broccoli	HH
broccoli, overwintering	H
Brussels sprouts	H
cabbage	H/HH
carrots	H/HH
cauliflower	H/HH
celery	HH
chard	H/HH
collard greens	H
corn salad (mache)	H
endive	HH
fennel	HH
garlic	H
kale	H
leeks	H
lettuce	HH
mesclun greens	HH
oats	HH
onions	H/HH
parsley	HH
parsnips	H
peas	HH
radishes	HH
rye	H
scallions	H
spinach	H
turnips	H
wheat	HH

H = Hardy (tolerates below-freezing temperatures)

HH = Half-hardy (withstands light frosts)

H/HH = Hardy or half-hardy, depending on selection

Opposite: Mesclun greens, including mizuna, mustard, and chard, are tolerant of light frosts.

10

HARVESTING & PREPARING FOR NEXT YEAR

The end of summer marks a time of plenty in the garden. If all has gone well, you are gathering armloads of apples, snipping fresh herbs to top every meal, and looking for someone willing to take another zucchini off your hands.

As the active growing season winds down, it can be tempting to be done with gardening for a few months. Believe me, I know: it has been go-time since early spring, and you want a break. But before you pack it in, devote a day or two to thinking about next year's garden.

This is also the time to prepare the garden for winter—to clean and put away pots and tools, and to save the seeds of the plants you want to grow again. First, however, is the fun part: the harvest.

Opposite: Harvesting your homegrown produce is supremely satisfying.

Finally. The moment you've been waiting for. Or is it? Is that pepper ready to pick, or could it use another week in the sun? Knowing when to harvest is more art than science, but some guidelines can help.

HARVESTING YOUR CROPS

Pick early and pick often. As tempting as it is to leave plump pods on the vine for all to admire, do not let ripe veggies hang around on the vine too long. Harvest them when they are young: older edibles tend to have a woody or leathery texture and can taste either bland or bitter. Harvest them when they are small: giant zucchinis and foot-long beans may look impressive, but they will be mealy, stringy, and tasteless. And, finally, harvest edibles frequently: thwarting your plants' attempts to produce seed just encourages them to try again . . . and again. Leaving ripe fruit on a plant will cause it to stop producing more.

Fruit and fruiting vegetables

Harvesting fruit is one of summer's great pleasures: collecting juicy strawberries for your breakfast; eating sun-warmed tomatoes right off the vine.

You can tell when most fruits and fruiting vegetables (which include cucurbits and most nightshades) are ready to harvest. Their color changes, often from green to red; they become softer; and they may become fragrant. Many tree fruits are ready to harvest if, when given a gentle twist, they drop into your palm. (Pears are a notable exception and should be picked when unripe.)

Mushrooms

Whether you are growing them in a specially prepared plot, on a log, or even indoors using a mushroom patch kit, most mushrooms can be harvested with a knife to make a clean cut at the bottom of the stem, or by twisting the stem. Eat only mushrooms that you have grown for that purpose; fungi often show up in our gardens, and although the presence of mushrooms indicates healthy soil, it is unwise to eat them unless you can positively identify them as safe (many are poisonous, after all).

Grains

The notion of a grain harvest conjures up some lovely bucolic images. You might not be doing all that threshing and winnowing on a large scale, but harvesting small amounts of grain at home can be a very satisfying experience. It is easy, too, if you have any familiarity with saving seed, because what we call grain is merely the seeds of these plants.

Harvest grain when the stalks have completely dried. The seeds should be dry and almost ready to drop on their own accord. But do not wait too long, or the seeds will begin to fall or rains will cause the grains to rot. Cut the tops off the plants and collect them in a cloth bag or bucket. (Quinoa can be harvested by grasping the stalk and stripping the grains off the top with an upward motion.) Rub the seed heads together in a sack to separate the grain from the chaff, or pour it onto a tarp; then, wearing heavy, clean shoes, scuff the grain against the ground with your feet. Remove the chaff using a screen or by blowing a fan or blow dryer on a cool setting over the seeds. Pick out any remaining debris, and spread the grains on trays to dry further (in the sun or indoors in a warm place) before storing them in an airtight container.

Herbs

Leafy herbs should be harvested frequently throughout the growing season by pinching back the most vigorous growth, which encourages them to become bushier and more prolific. Pick herbs just before eating for the most intense flavor. Large quantities can be dried or frozen at the end of the season. Chop fresh herbs, place them in ice cube trays, top up with water, and freeze for later use. Or cut off the stems of perennial herbs at almost soil level and hang the cut plants to dry in a cool, dry place.

. . . .

Opposite: Hulless barley shows it is ready for harvesting.

Leafy and root vegetables

Harvest the outer leaves of leafy greens such as chard, lettuce, and kale as soon as plants are large enough to spare a few, or treat them as a cut-and-come again crop and cut them back to an inch (2.5 cm) above the ground. More leaves will usually appear for a second and third harvest. Like most vegetables, lettuce and salad greens are best when harvested young; overly mature lettuce is bitter and tough.

It can be difficult to judge when root crops are ripe for harvesting. Beets and carrots often start to poke out of the ground when they are ready for harvest. Garlic, bulb onions, and potatoes indicate readiness through their dying leaves and stems.

Above: Heirloom tomatoes such as 'Purple Calabash' look nothing like the average supermarket variety.

Opposite: Select seeds from the best plants with the most desirable characteristics.

SAVING SEEDS

Saving seeds has recently gone from simply being a thrifty mode of plant propagation to a defiant political statement. Although the original motivations are still more than valid—to save money by not having to buy new seed every year, and to select the seeds from plants that perform well under local conditions—more than ever, people are saving seeds for other reasons.

Hybrids and heirlooms

The majority of commercially sold seeds are hybrids, an often deliberate cross between two different parent plants. Hybrids are selected for traits desired by the breeder. That might be flavor, but in industrial agriculture, hybrids are judged by their ability to store well or withstand long-distance shipping. Hybrid seeds, which are identified F1 (first filial generation) on the packet, are genetically identical. Growers must repeat the original cross year after year through controlled pollination. As a result, the seeds of hybrid plants may be sterile or may revert to characteristics of one of the parent plants. Because one can never be certain what they will produce, hybrid seeds aren't usually saved by most gardeners; instead, they buy new seed every year.

Open-pollinated (or OP) plants are the other side of the coin. These plants are pollinated by wind, bees, and other pollinators and, in many cases, produce viable seed that will produce a plant just like its parent. (Cucurbits and other families that readily cross-pollinate are a major exception, however.) In fact, the plants grown from OP seeds you have saved may even perform better than the original plants the year before, because they have started to adjust to the conditions of your own little microclimate. Although F1 seeds are static, OP seeds adapt. This preservation of a diverse plant gene pool is one of the major reasons for growing open-pollinated edibles (being able to save your own seeds is the other).

Heirloom vegetables and fruits are always open-pollinated. Although no one can quite agree on how old a particular selection needs to be to be considered an heirloom, most of these plants were in existence prior to World War II and the advent of industrial agriculture. Some are centuries old.

Heirloom edibles are not grown in the large-scale commercial monocultures that supply the majority of supermarket produce, but they are often incredibly flavorful and weirdly beautiful. Growing and saving heirloom seed helps to keep these older types of edibles alive and pushes back against the increasing homogenization of our food supply.

So, bottom line, should you avoid hybrid seed? My personal take on it is an unequivocal "mostly." Here's the thing—hybrid plants can be quite useful. Some have been bred for disease-resistance; others are bred to ripen early or to take up less space. These are all good things. But if hybrids were all we grew, we would be participating in the extinction of older open-pollinated selections. So although there is nothing wrong with buying the occasional F1 seed, your aim should be to grow mostly OP seed. Besides, being able to harvest items that cannot be found in grocery stores is half the fun of growing your own food. Seek out rare and unusual plants through seed-saving organizations or reputable seed companies that trade in organic, non-GMO seeds. And of course, whenever possible, save your own.

Collecting and storing seeds

Saving the seeds of some vegetables, such as peas and peppers, is straightforward: simply collect, clean, dry, and store. Others, such as corn and cucumber, are a little more complicated, requiring separation from other plants to prevent random cross-pollination (and thus producing seed that does not accurately reproduce the parent plant). Another class of vegetables, which includes carrots and cabbages, not only requires separation, but needs more than a year to produce seed.

When you are starting out in seed-saving, try seeds of open-pollinated beans, dill, cilantro, lettuce, peas, peppers, and tomatoes. These edibles offer your best chance for success, especially if you grow only one type of each crop.

. . . .

Opposite: Dill seeds drop easily when they are dry; cut off the seed heads and carefully store them in a paper bag until they are completely dry. Then tuck them away for next year.

Below: Pea seeds are some of the easiest to save. Let the pods dry on the vines before removing the seeds.

CUCURBITS: THE GREAT CROSS-POLLINATORS

Many vegetables will cross-pollinate with others within their species, effectively creating their own hybrids. Although this will not affect the current year's harvest, the fruit will have seeds that will be sterile or, if planted the next year, that will produce offspring that looks nothing like the parent. Seed companies get around this natural tendency by separating different cross-pollinating plants by at least 1 mile (1.6 km) or by erecting a physical barrier between plants to maintain purity.

Cucurbits commonly cross-pollinate, so if you are growing more than one type of *Cucurbita pepo* (acorn squash and pumpkin, for example), you can pretty much count on the fact that seeds from both plants will produce funky offspring. If you want to save seeds, replace one of the above with Hubbard squash, a type of *C. maxima*—same genus, but different species. They will not cross-pollinate and will produce viable seeds (that is, as long as none of your neighbors are also growing squash).

If you feel lucky, try saving the seeds of OP corn, cucumber, melon, radish, and squash, providing you are growing only one type. (Commercial growers separate these plants by at least half a mile, or 800m; less for corn.)

Whichever seeds you decide to save, your first item of business is to identify the plants that produced solidly or the earliest, or that resisted disease the best. In essence, seed-saving makes you a backyard plant breeder, allowing you to continue the lineage of a strong performer—so choose wisely.

○ **Saving seeds from nonfruiting herbs and vegetables.** In spring or early summer, gardeners usually try to prevent plants from bolting, but for end-of-season seed-saving purposes, we want the plants to bolt. Bolting occurs when cool-season crops such as radishes and lettuce decide it's high time to make some babies already. They send up a stalk, which grows tall and eventually flowers. We collect the seeds from the flowers or pods produced, and everyone's happy.

Saving these types of seeds is easiest if you allow them to ripen and dry on the plant. Then you can clip them off, brush off any bugs or dirt, and then tuck the heads into paper bags until they are completely dry. Sometimes it's better to cut off the seedpods or flower heads before they are fully ripe. Strong winds and wet weather can scatter seeds and cause rot, so if nasty weather is imminent, cut off the seedheads and hang them upside down in a dry, well-ventilated spot. Tie a paper bag around each seedhead to collect the seeds as they drop. Once the seedheads are completely dry, tease the seeds from their pods.

○ **Saving seeds from fruiting vegetables.** The seeds from fruiting vegetables are harvested wet. The fruits should be picked when fully ripe, cut open, and the seeds removed. Spoon the seeds (and inevitable pulp) into a mesh colander or sieve for washing. Try to remove all the pulp. Some seeds, such as those of peppers and melons, are easily cleaned; just set them aside on a plate or towel to dry before storing.

Tomato seeds require special treatment; they are protected by a growth-inhibiting gel coating that must be removed before you store them. Cut the tomato in half, scoop out and rinse the seeds, and place them in a mason jar with a cup (237 ml) or so of water. Do not seal the jar; cover the opening with cheesecloth or a towel. Place the jar in a warm, out-of-the-way location (the mixture is going to reek). Start checking for signs of fermentation after a couple days. When you see a layer of mold growing on the surface, the seeds are ready. Scoop off the top layer of mold, immature seeds, and other gunk; viable seeds will have settled on the bottom. Rinse them under running water, and then transfer them to a plate or towel to dry.

○ **Storing seeds.** Seal seeds in labeled paper envelopes or small, airtight jars (paper envelopes should be enclosed in an airtight container), and then stash them in the refrigerator or another cool, dry place. Heat and humidity spell certain death for most seeds. Stored properly, many seeds will last for up to three or more years. (Alliums and parsnips are an exception; sow these seeds within one year.)

Opposite: Mint is easily propagated by cuttings.

MAKING NEW PLANTS BY
TAKING CUTTINGS

Not all edibles are best propagated by seed. Woody herbs and shrubs are often propagated by cuttings, and fruit tree scions (twig cuttings) are grafted onto desirable rootstocks. Although grafting is an art best left to experts and enthusiastic hobbyists, taking cuttings requires no more than a sharp knife and a little know-how.

Many woody and soft-stemmed plants can be propagated by cutting a stem and placing it in water or soil. You might have noticed a cut flower that grew little white roots from its stem; that's the magic (and ease) of propagating plants in this way.

Soft-stemmed herbs such as mint and basil readily grow roots when placed in water. Take a cutting by snipping off the top 3 to 6 in. (8 to 15 cm) from a lower side shoot just below a pair of leaves. Remove the bottom leaves and place the cutting in a glass of water. Change the water every couple of days. Roots should appear within two weeks. The cutting can then be gently transplanted into potting soil.

In the same way, you can take cuttings of the new spring growth of woody-stemmed herbs, such as rosemary and sage, and shrubs such as blueberry. Instead of rooting them in water, however, place the cuttings in potting soil. You can dip the cuttings in rooting hormone to help encourage root formation, but doing so is not always necessary. Keep the pots well watered, out of direct sun, and enclosed in a plastic bag to hold humidity (the bag should not touch the plant's leaves). The cuttings will root in four to six weeks.

Above: Basil roots easily in water.

PREPARING THE GARDEN FOR WINTER

At some point in late summer or autumn, depending on your locale, it will be time to prepare for the winter. The main objectives of the big fall cleanup are to protect your soil from erosion caused by winter rains and to remove opportunities for pests and diseases to proliferate.

Remove plant debris

After the last of your summer vegetables have been harvested, pull out the plants, plus any weeds and fallen leaves, and add them to the compost. To avoid cursing yourself with a new generation of problems, do not compost diseased or pest-ridden plants, perennial weeds, or weed seeds. Those should go in the trash. Leave hardy or half-hardy plants in the ground and continue to harvest edibles as long as you can.

Cover the soil

If you have been nurturing along some transplants for your fall and winter harvest, plant these as soon as possible. If you didn't get around to starting or buying transplants, sow a cover crop (green mulch) or spread on a layer of compost or leaf mulch to reduce erosion and improve the soil.

Protect tender plants

Unless you are lucky enough to live where the ground never freezes, you need to protect nonhardy or marginally hardy perennials from the ravages of winter. This is especially true of container plantings; these plants are less insulated from the cold than in-ground plants.

Tender plants should be lifted and brought indoors for the winter. Potted herbs such as rosemary will make do on a bright windowsill; larger plants can ride out the winter in an unheated garage, as long as the temperature stays above freezing. Borderline hardy plants can be protected with a thick layer of mulch, or they can be wrapped with burlap.

Clean and store tools

Collect empty containers and remove any remaining dirt or plant debris. Scrub them out with soapy water, or leave them to soak overnight in a 9:1 solution of water and hydrogen peroxide.

Collect stakes and tomato cages and store them out of the rain or snow. Gardening tools can also be cleaned at this time. At the least, wipe them down with soapy water, and then dry them thoroughly before storing. Pruning shears should be sterilized with a quick dip in a 1:2 hydrogen peroxide and water bath to prevent the spread of disease. The heads of shovels, hoes, and other tools with metal parts can be cleaned and oiled in one go: mix some oil into a bucket of coarse sand and poke in your shovels and pruning shears. Wipe off the sand and your tools are ready for winter hibernation. And so are you.

Reflect

Once the garden has been put to bed, you can relax and reflect on your successes. If this was your first successful garden, you deserve congratulations! If your experience was like mine, it was interesting, motivating, and, above all, satisfying. If your garden (or its produce) failed to live up to your expectations, take this time to reassess.

What crops tasted the best? Which crops were the most carefree? How can you replicate your successes?

Which crops were planted too late, didn't get enough sun, or were plagued by pests? What are you going to do about it next time?

What vegetables did you grow but not eat—because, after all, you don't really like eggplant/cabbage/kale? Should you have planted more of another type of vegetable?

What did you see in other gardeners' gardens, seed catalogues, books, or magazines, that you want to try next year?

I believe that, no matter how much you read, research, or plan, gardening is a lifelong learning process—a (mostly) joyful experiment in trial and error. Like me, you will make plenty of errors, and that's okay. Some years will be incredible—you'll harvest tons of perfectly delicious, blemish-free produce and smugly admit that you're a natural at this gardening thing. Other years your garden will limp along, crippled by poor weather, pests, and your two-week vacation, during which your neighbor failed to water as promised. Shake it off. Get back out there. Celebrate your successes, learn from your mistakes, and, above all, enjoy the process.

EDIBLES FROM A TO Z

From apples to zucchini, details on when, how, and what to plant in your small space are included here. Use this part of the book as a quick-reference resource when you need info, pronto. You can also use this information as a planning tool and a source of inspiration while you are developing a planting scheme for the new season.

Not all of the edibles mentioned are suited to growing in containers or in tiny spaces. They are included, however, because some gardeners might choose to devote all their available space to growing one fantastic, stately artichoke plant. Others might have a bit more room and decide to give a full-sized fruit tree a try. For those looking for the ultimate edibles for small spaces, look for the Top Pick symbol. These are the crops that, in my experience, make the best choices for truly small gardens.

Each listing includes recommendations for a number of great cultivars; I believe, however, that you can find the best edibles to grow by talking to other gardeners in your area. A tomato that performs amazingly in one area might be a flop in another, so ask at a favorite nursery or talk to neighbors for their recommendations.

Finally, a note about hardiness: for perennial plants, hardiness zones indicate the temperature range in which a particular plant will thrive. However, not all cultivars within a species will necessarily be hardy to the zone indicated; great variation can exist in the hardiness of different cultivars. In addition, container-grown plants will be less hardy than those grown in the ground—keep that in mind when you are choosing what to grow and where to grow it.

Opposite: Pumpkins are not usually considered compact plants for a small space, but they sure pack a punch in the garden and are well suited to edible landscapes.

APPLE

Malus domestica
Deciduous tree, hardy in zones 3–9

If you thought you couldn't have an orchard on a balcony, think again. With dwarfing rootstocks that make it possible to grow trees as small as 4 ft. (1.2 m) tall and 2 ft. (60 cm) wide, pruning and training techniques that create espaliered trees that grow low and flat against a fence or wall, and grafting methods that produce three or more types of apple on one tree, the apple is the ultimate small-space fruit tree. The only catch is that most apples will not self-pollinate, meaning you must plant at least two trees of different types (or one grafted tree with multiple apple selections) or you won't get any fruit.

Start: Apples do not reproduce accurately from seed; instead, they are grown by grafting a scion (the trunk and upper part of the tree, or a branch of a tree) onto a rootstock, which determines the tree's final size and hardiness. Trees can be transplanted from fall through spring. Spring is better for those in cold climates; warm-climate gardeners can plant in the fall. Formative pruning should also be done in the late fall or winter. Many apples, especially those grown on dwarfing rootstocks, should be staked.

Grow: Place trees in full sun, in moist, well-drained soil. Apples do not actually require pruning, but it can help produce a desirable shape and improve fruit production. Spray with a horticultural oil in late winter to kill overwintering pests if they were problems in the past. In spring, mulch with compost, avoiding the trunk and root crown area, and scratch a complete organic fertilizer into the soil. This is also the time to hang codling moth traps and apply sticky tree bands if codling moths are a problem in your area. Thinning—removing fruit while it is still developing—allows the remaining fruit to grow larger, improves next year's production, and reduces the chance that limbs will break under the weight of a heavy crop. Thin apples when they are 1 in. (2.5 cm) in diameter, leaving only one apple per cluster. Thinning is especially crucial in new trees; strip all blossoms and fruit from trees during their first year.

Harvest: Dwarf apples take two or more years to produce a good harvest; standard types may take up to five years to produce fruit. Trees are usually at least one year old when you purchase them at the nursery. Apples are ready to harvest in late summer or early fall, depending on the type. Ripe apples will come away from the tree with a gentle twist.

Tips: Choose an apple tree based on your climate, your available space, and your eating preferences. Multiple-grafted trees are great small-space options because they are self-fertile—more than one type of apple is grafted onto one rootstock, so you need only one tree—and you get to try a few different types of apples. Alternatively, plant two or more columnar selections—dwarf trees with very short branches and a bottlebrush appearance. They measure only 2 ft. (60 cm) wide and are often less than 6 ft. (1.8 m) tall.

In containers: Dwarf and columnar apples do well in containers; choose a large container or half-barrel at least 2 ft. (60 cm) deep.

Problems: Aphids, codling moth, fire blight, plum curculio, powdery mildew, scab.

Popular selections: In small spaces, choose trees on dwarfing rootstocks such as M27, M26, Mark, or M9. Talk to a reputable nursery or orchardist for recommendations for your area. If you can have only one tree, make sure it is a self-pollinating cultivar such as 'Granny Smith' or 'Golden Delicious' (though even these trees will produce better if cross-pollinated with another type of apple). In areas with mild winters, choose cultivars that do not require long, cold winters to set fruit, such as 'Dorsett Golden' or 'Anna'. Other popular apples include 'Bramley's Seedling', 'Northern Spy', and 'Liberty' for pies and cooking; and 'Cox's Orange Pippin', 'Fiesta', 'Honeycrisp', and 'Gala' for fresh eating. 'Scarlet Sentinel', 'Golden Sentinel', and 'Northpole' are popular columnar cultivars.

Opposite: Extremely amenable to espalier and other small-space pruning techniques, apples are the ultimate fruit tree for small gardens.

APRICOT

Prunus armeniaca
Deciduous tree, hardy in zones 5–9

With their showy pink or white blossoms, apricots make beautiful specimen trees for the small garden. Late spring frosts are the major hindrance to apricot growing; frost kills the blossoms, reducing fruit yield. If late frosts are an issue in your area, look for apricots that bloom later in the spring. Unlike apples, most apricots are self-pollinating, although a tree will produce more fruit if grown close to another type of apricot. Dwarf trees can be grown in containers.

Start: Bare-root or container-grown trees can be transplanted from fall through spring. Spring is better for those in cold climates; gardeners in warmer climates can plant them in the fall.

Grow: In full sun and a sheltered location, in moist, well-drained soil. Train into an open-vase shape or espalier into a fan shape, pruning after the tree has flowered. Thinning—removing fruit while it is still developing—allows the remaining fruit to grow larger, improves next year's production, and reduces the chance that limbs will break under the weight of a heavy crop. Thin apricots when they are small, leaving 2 to 3 in. (5 to 8 cm) between fruits— even more when the tree is young.

Harvest: In midsummer to late summer, once the fruit is even in color and slightly soft.

Tips: Even if you choose a late-blooming apricot, unexpected frosts can cause damage. Protect blossoms from impending frosts by covering the tree with a light sheet or cloth.

In containers: Choose a dwarf tree and a large container or half-barrel at least 20 in. (50 cm) deep.

Problems: Bacterial canker, brown rot, leafhoppers, mites, nematodes, powdery mildew, verticillium wilt.

Popular selections: Many apricots are available in both standard and dwarfing rootstocks; be sure to choose a dwarfing rootstock such as 'Pixie'. Also choose self-fertile types that bloom after your area's average last frost date. 'Harglow' and 'Tilton' are self-pollinating and late-blooming varieties; 'Royal Blenheim' is the classic semi-dwarf California apricot—good for areas with mild winters.

ARTICHOKE

Cynara scolymus
Tender perennial, grown as an annual in areas with cold winters, hardy to zone 7

These large, tender perennials produce gorgeous thistlelike flower buds that are coveted for their delicious hearts. Artichokes make beautiful focal points in any garden; however, their large size makes them less than suitable for very small spaces.

Start: Start indoors 8 to 12 weeks before the last frost; transplant outside after the last frost. Space plants 3 ft. (1 m) apart.

Grow: In a sheltered, full-sun location with well-drained, fertile soil. Artichokes are heavy feeders; amend the soil with compost prior to planting and fertilize with a potassium-rich fertilizer throughout the growing season.

Harvest: In summer, cut flower buds 2 to 3 in. (5 to 8 cm) below the base just before they begin to open.

Tips: In areas with mild winters, protect plants with a thick layer of mulch and try growing as perennials; artichokes produce best in their second year.

In containers: Since artichokes can grow to 3 to 5 ft. (1 to 1.5 m) tall and wide, they are not great candidates for container growing. If you are determined, however, grow one plant per half barrel–sized container and fertilize regularly.

Problems: Slugs.

Popular selections: 'Green Globe' and 'Imperial Star' will produce buds in their first year.

ARUGULA, see Lettuce and salad greens

ASIAN GREENS

TOP PICK

Brassica juncea and **B. rapa**
Hardy and half-hardy, cool-season annuals

Asian greens is a catchall term for leafy greens in the brassica family. They are often grown as a cut-and-come-again crop, harvested young and eaten raw in salads, or, when larger, tossed in a stir-fry. They include a variety of leafy mustards, mizuna, komatsuna, and mibuna, and sometimes bok choy (a type of Chinese cabbage). You can often find a blend of these seeds packaged together and sold as Asian Greens or Spicy Mix.

Start: Direct sow in early spring, succession sowing every few weeks until the summer heat hits. Sow again in late summer for a fall harvest. Scatter seeds evenly across moist soil and cover them with a thin layer of soil—or scratch seeds into the surface.

Grow: In full sun, in fertile, moist, well-drained soil. Asian greens enjoy full sun when the weather is cool, but some shade is helpful in preventing bolting during warm weather. Add lime to acidic soils prior to planting and amend with manure, compost, or a complete organic fertilizer.

Harvest: When plants are 4 to 6 in. (10 to 15 cm) tall, cut back to 1 or 2 in. (2.5 to 5 cm) above the soil surface. Leaves will resprout, providing several more harvests. Harvest greens frequently for the best flavor.

Tips: Asian greens are attractive additions to the cool-season garden and for edging containers or beds. Some are hardy and will overwinter in all but the coldest climates.

Problems: Aphids, flea beetles.

In containers: Good even in small (6 in., or 15 cm, deep) containers.

Popular selections: Mizuna has deeply serrated green leaves and is quite mild; 'Red Giant' mustard has large, burgundy leaves—it tastes mild when harvested in cool weather and tangy when harvested in the heat.

ASPARAGUS

Asparagus officinalis
Cool-season perennial, hardy in zones 2–9

An asparagus bed is a long-term commitment. This long-lived perennial needs a lot of space—growing up to 5 ft. (1.5 m) tall and just as wide—as well as time to mature. But once started, it produces one of the earliest and most delicious spring vegetables.

Start: Purchase one-year-old crowns (roots). Transplant them outside after the last frost.

Grow: In full sun or part shade. Plant crowns in a deep (12 in., or 30 cm) trench or hole amended with manure or compost, spacing plants 18 in. (45 cm) apart. Gradually add more soil as shoots emerge, without covering the tips. Mulch with compost or manure every spring, prior to the emergence of shoots.

Harvest: Do not harvest spears until the third spring, allowing the resulting leafy fronds to nourish the roots. In the third year, harvest spears by snapping or cutting them off at ground level when they are 5 to 10 in. (12.5 to 25 cm) tall. Stop harvesting when the emerging spears start to grow thinner; allow them to grow into tall, ferny foliage that will support next year's harvest. Remove the foliage in fall to prevent asparagus beetles from overwintering.

Tips: White asparagus, expensive to buy in stores, is simply regular asparagus that has been kept out of the sun. Grow your own by covering the growing spears with mulch or plastic pots.

In containers: Not recommended.

Problems: Asparagus beetles, fusarium wilt, rust.

Popular selections: Choose male hybrids (which produce the best spears) such as 'Jersey Knight', 'Jersey Giant', or UC 157.

BASIL

Ocimum spp.
Tender annual

 BEANS

Phaseolus spp. and *Glycine max*
Warm-season annual

A mainstay of Italian and Asian cooking, basil is a beautiful and hard-working addition to any edible garden. When grown with tomatoes, it is said to improve their flavor; basil also repels aphids and mites.

Start: Start seeds indoors 4 to 6 weeks prior to the last frost, or direct sow seeds once the soil has warmed. Space plants 12 in. (30 cm) apart.

Grow: In full to part sun, in a warm, sheltered location. Soil should be rich, consistently moist, and well-drained. Pinch out the growing tip beginning when the plant is about 4 in. (10 cm) tall to encourage bushy growth and inhibit flowering.

Harvest: Harvest regularly, pinching off the tips of the stems. Best eaten fresh, basil can also be frozen, dried, or preserved in oil.

Tips: If you have a bright, sunny windowsill available, move your pot of basil indoors at the end of summer to prolong the harvest.

In containers: Excellent in containers at least 4 in. (10 cm) deep.

Problems: Slugs, verticillium wilt.

Popular selections: Italian selections include the classics for pesto: 'Sweet Basil' and 'Genovese'. 'Purple Ruffles' and 'Cinnamon' are beautifully ornamental. 'Pesto Perpetuo' is an unusual, creamy white and green variegated variety that rarely goes to seed.

Beans should be on everyone's must-grow list: no supermarket bean can compare to the taste of homegrown, fresh-picked beans. They are one of the easiest vegetables to start from seed and are equally easy to grow. In fact, the toughest part is often choosing which type to plant.

Beans are a diverse group. Some are climbers; others are short and bushy. But the biggest distinction among them is the stage at which they are harvested. Snap beans, also known as green, wax, or string beans, are harvested young and eaten whole, including the pod. Shelling beans, also called horticultural beans, are harvested and shelled when the beans have swelled in the pods but are still tender. Beans for drying are harvested after the pods have dried on the plant. Some cross-over occurs between the groups: some snap and shelling beans can be dried, while some dry beans, if picked early enough, can be eaten as shell beans or even green beans. (Note that fava beans, which are broad beans, are not included in this discussion and are covered in the section on broad beans.)

Start: Direct sow after the soil has really warmed up—usually in late spring. Seeds will rot in cool, wet soil. Plant seeds 4 to 8 in. (10 to 20 cm) apart in moistened soil, and avoid watering until they have sprouted. In areas with wet, cool springs, start beans indoors and plant them out after the weather has stabilized—but be extremely gentle when transplanting because they don't like to be moved. Using a legume inoculant on seeds or in the planting hole prior to planting encourages healthy growth by introducing beneficial microorganisms that increase the availability of nitrogen in your soil. You can find inoculants online or at garden centers.

Grow: In full sun, in well-drained soil. Bush beans do not require support, but climbers need a teepee or another vertical support. Set up supports prior to planting to avoid inadvertently damaging the growing roots.

Opposite: Sweet basil is a beautiful plant if pinched back to encourage bushiness.

Harvest: Harvest frequently (daily is best) to encourage greater production, preferably when the plant's leaves are dry to avoid spreading disease. Pick snap and other beans eaten in the pod when they are small and still tender; after the seeds start to swell, the pods become stringy. Shelling beans, lima beans, and soybeans can be harvested after the seeds have swelled but are still green and tender. Dried beans are ready for harvest when the pods are dry and rattle when shaken.

Tips: In small spaces, pole and runner beans make excellent use of vertical space. You can also train these climbers over trellises to provide shade to heat-sensitive crops. Many beans have pretty flowers or interesting pods in colors ranging from purple to yellow (wax) or even striped.

In containers: Bush and dwarf types do well in containers that are at least 9 in. (22 cm) deep; climbers prefer large tubs or half-barrels.

Problems: Aphids, bacterial blight, leafhoppers, Mexican bean beetle, rust, slugs.

Popular selections: Dry beans (*Phaseolus vulgaris*): Red-speckled 'Jacob's Cattle' is extremely popular; flavorful 'Black Turtle' can also be eaten as a snap bean. Lima beans (*P. lunatus*): 'Henderson Bush' is compact; 'Christmas' is a pretty climber. Runner beans (*P. coccineus*): 'Scarlet Runner' is an attractive heirloom cultivar; 'White Emergo' is a white-flowering cultivar. Shelling beans (*P. vulgaris*): 'Chevrier' is a classic flageolet bush cultivar; 'Tongue of Fire' can also be eaten as a snap bean. Snap beans (*P. vulgaris*): 'Kentucky Wonder', 'Blue Lake', and 'Romano' are classics, available as bush or pole growers. 'Golden Child' is a wax (yellow) bean well suited for containers; 'Royal Burgundy' produces purple pods on a bush plant. Soybeans (*Glycine max*): 'Early Hakucho' produces early; 'Sayamusume' has great flavor.

TOP PICK

BEETS

Beta vulgaris
Half-hardy, cool-season biennials grown as annuals

With their attractive and edible leaves, delicious roots, and ability to produce in less than full sun, beets make an excellent crop for beginners. Also known as beetroot, beets are available in a variety of root shapes and colors beyond basic beet red.

Start: Direct sow at the time of last frost, succession sowing every 2 to 3 weeks until midsummer. Space 1 to 2 in. (2.5 to 5 cm) apart, thinning to 5 in. (12.5 cm) apart when plants are 2 in. (5 cm) tall.

Grow: In fertile, well-drained, consistently moist soil with added compost. Beets grow well in full sun or part shade.

Harvest: Start by harvesting and eating the thinned seedlings, and then progress to snipping off the occasional outer leaf as the plants develop. Roots can be harvested in 45 to 100 days, depending on the type. They are best harvested young; older beets become woody.

Tips: Keep beets well watered; dry soil causes roots to become woody or split. They may bolt in hot weather, so harvest them before the heat hits or provide some shade.

In containers: The smaller, rounded selections are best for container growing. Choose containers with a depth of at least 10 in. (25 cm).

Problems: Flea beetles, leaf miners, slugs.

Popular selections: Heirloom cultivar 'Chioggia' produces red-and-white–striped roots; 'Touchstone Gold' has orange roots and gold-veined leaves; hybrid 'Red Ace' starts out quickly in spring and can be harvested year-round in areas with mild winters.

Opposite: Beets, shade-tolerant and easy to grow, make an attractive container crop.

BLACKBERRIES AND BLACKBERRY HYBRIDS

Rubus spp.
Perennial cane fruit, hardy in zones 5–9

Blackberries are one of the quintessential summer fruits. Although you can often find them growing wild, cultivating them at home allows you to select a thornless type or choose one of the many hybrids available. Blackberry canes are either trailing and thicket-forming or erect and somewhat self-supporting. The blackberry hybrids, which include boysenberry, loganberry, tayberry, youngberry, and dewberry, are usually in the trailing class. Their canes are long and vinelike and should be tied to a support. The erect types are shorter and do not require trellising; these are also more cold-tolerant. Don't expect berries your first summer: blackberries produce fruit on two-year-old canes.

Start: Purchase bare-root or container-grown plants. Transplant them from fall through spring. Spring is better for those in cold climates; gardeners in warm climates can plant in the fall.

Grow: In full or part sun in a sheltered location. Soil should be rich in organic matter, moist, and well-drained. Space erect types 2 ft. (60 cm) apart; trailing types require 5 ft. (152 cm) or more between plants. Plant against a trellis, fence, or wire support, and tie up new fruit-bearing canes as they appear, starting in the second year. After harvest, cut back the canes that produced fruit that summer to the ground, leaving the newer canes to produce fruit for next year. For protection against extreme winter temperatures, bend the canes to the ground and mulch with straw for the winter.

Harvest: Early to late summer, depending on the selection.

Tips: If kept in check, these vertical growers do not take up too much space. Train them up the side of the garage, in the back alley, or along any fence.

In containers: You can grow blackberries in large (half-barrel–sized) containers, but these vigorous plants are more suited to in-ground gardening.

Problems: Birds, powdery mildew, verticillium wilt.

Popular selections: 'Chester' is a semi-erect, thornless cultivar that is extremely cold-tolerant; 'Triple Crown' is a trailing, thornless berry that is also hardy; 'Ouachita' is an erect, thornless plant that ripens early and is suited to warmer climates. Also try hybrids such as the loganberry, a cross between blackberry and raspberry, and boysenberry, a cross between blackberry, loganberry, and raspberry.

BLUEBERRIES AND CRANBERRIES

Vaccinium spp.
Deciduous perennial shrubs, hardy in zones 3–9

With their pretty spring flowers, attractive summer berries, and brilliant fall color, blueberries and cranberries make excellent shrubs for the edible landscape or ornamental border. Huckleberries and lingonberries are also members of this genus. For all, the major growing requirement is acidic soil— pH 5.0 or lower. Plant more than one type to ensure cross-pollination and good fruit production.

Start: Purchase bare-root or container-grown plants, or take a cutting from a friend's plant. Transplant from fall through spring. Spring is better for those in cold climates; warm-climate gardeners can plant in the fall. Space plants 4 ft. (1.2 m) apart.

Grow: In full or part sun, in well-drained, moist, acidic soil. Amend soil with pine shavings, pine needles, peat, coffee grounds, or sulfur prior to planting. If your soil naturally tends toward neutral (pH 7.0) or alkaline (above pH 7.0), grow these shrubs in large containers and provide suitable soil. Water regularly, and mulch in the spring, starting in year two. During the first year, strip off any flower buds to force the plant to put energy into root development. Starting in year three, practice regular annual pruning.

Harvest: Starting the second year, harvest berries in early summer through fall, depending on the plant. Blueberries will be deep blue and sweet; cranberries ripen to bright red.

Tips: Lowbush blueberries are the smallest, at under 2 ft. (60 cm) tall. Rabbiteye blueberry shrubs can reach 10 ft. (3 m) or taller. Lowbush blueberries are extremely cold hardy but do not do well in warm-winter areas, because they require a cold, dormant period. Highbush blueberries are the most flexible, thriving in a range of climates.

In containers: Good in containers at least 20 in. (50 cm) deep as long as the soil is acidic.

Problems: Birds, botrytis blight, powdery mildew.

Popular selections: Blueberries: 'Northsky' is an extremely hardy lowbush blueberry suited to container growing; 'Blueray' and 'Bluecrop' are hardy and vigorous highbush types; 'Powder Blue' is a late-ripening rabbiteye cultivar suited to areas with warm winters. Cranberries: 'Ben Lear' is an early-ripening cultivar; 'Stevens' is a widely grown commercial hybrid. Others: Try evergreen or deciduous huckleberries (*Vaccinium ovatum* and *V. parvifolium*) and lingonberries (*V. vitis-idaea*).

BOK CHOY, see Chinese cabbage

BROAD BEANS

Vicia faba
Hardy, cool-season annual

Broad beans, also known as fava or horse beans, are unusual because they are cool-season beans. Whereas snap and shelling beans are decidedly heat-seeking, broad beans are hardy in all but the coldest climates. These large plants are useful as an overwintering crop. Some people, particularly those with Mediterranean ancestry, are strongly allergic to broad beans.

Start: Direct sow in late fall or early spring. Space 10 in. (25 cm) apart.

Grow: In full sun, in well-drained soil. Pinch back tips to encourage bushiness.

Harvest: When pods are plump and tender for shelling, or allow to dry on the plant for dried beans. The leaves are also edible.

Tips: Broad beans are often used as a trap crop because they are irresistible to aphids.

In containers: It is possible to grow broad beans in large containers; however, their size makes them more suited to in-ground gardening.

Problems: Aphids, bacterial blight, leafhoppers, Mexican bean beetle, rust, slugs.

Popular selections: 'Broad Windsor' is a classic; 'Optica' is compact.

BROCCOLI

Brassica oleracea var. botrytis
Half-hardy, cool-season annual

Broccoli is a cool-season annual that produces clusters of edible flowers. Some form a single head, but others produce smaller heads on multiple side shoots.

Start: Start seeds indoors 4 to 6 weeks before the last frost date, or direct sow in the garden at that time. Space 12 in. (30 cm) apart. Plant again in midsummer for a fall or winter harvest.

Grow: Broccoli can be challenging for the beginner. It requires full sun, consistent moisture, and rich, fertile soil. Amend the soil with manure, compost, or a complete organic fertilizer before planting. In acidic soils, broccoli will benefit from the addition of lime.

Harvest: Cut stems with a sharp knife before the flower heads open. Once the main head is cut, secondary stems will develop; keep picking broccoli heads to encourage production.

Tips: Try hardy sprouting broccoli, which produces small heads on long shoots, for your winter garden. To reduce problems from pests and disease, do not grow broccoli in the same place in consecutive years.

In containers: Choose a compact type suited to container growing and a container at least 10 in. (25 cm) deep.

Problems: Aphids, cabbage maggot, caterpillars, clubroot, cutworms, leaf miners, mildew.

Popular selections: 'Everest' is a good container option; 'Natalino' is a compact Romanesco cultivar. Purple-sprouting broccoli produces a multitude of colorful heads.

BRUSSELS SPROUTS

Brassica oleracea **var.** *gemmifera*
Half-hardy, cool-season annual

These cool-season curiosities are not well suited for very small spaces, but they are wonderful eaten fresh from the garden after a touch of frost.

Start: Start seeds indoors 6 weeks prior to the last frost for your area, or in midsummer for the winter garden. Set transplants 20 in. (50 cm) apart.

Grow: In full sun, in fertile, well-drained soil. Keep plants evenly moist and well mulched. Brussels sprouts do best in cooler temperatures.

Harvest: Slice or snap off well-formed sprouts before they begin to open, starting at the bottom of the stalk. Upper sprouts will continue to mature. If possible, harvest after a frost for sweeter sprouts.

Tips: To force the sprouts to mature at once, pinch out the top of the stalk after the lowest sprouts have reached ½ to 1 in. (1 to 2.5 cm) in size; you'll get a full stalk of mature sprouts in a couple of weeks.

In containers: Suited to large containers or half-barrels.

Problems: Aphids, cabbage maggot, caterpillars, clubroot, cutworms, mildew.

Popular selections: 'Oliver' is vigorous and compact; 'Red Bull' has attractive red foliage and sprouts.

CABBAGE

Brassica oleracea **var.** *capitata*
Half-hardy, cool-season biennial grown as an annual

It might seem silly to grow such a cheaply available crop at home, but cabbage can be quite a striking addition to a veggie patch or ornamental bed. Several types of cabbages can be grown year-round in most climates.

Start: For summer harvests, start indoors 4 weeks prior to the last frost. For fall and winter harvests, start indoors or outdoors in midsummer. Start overwintering cabbages indoors in midsummer, transplanting out in late summer; harvest the following spring. Space plants 24 to 36 in. (60 to 90 cm) apart.

Grow: In full sun, in well-drained, consistently moist, fertile soil amended with abundant organic matter. Cabbage prefers cooler temperatures and can benefit from shade during hot weather. Add lime to acidic soils prior to planting. A dose of complete organic fertilizer can be beneficial, because cabbage is a heavy feeder.

Harvest: Cut off well-formed heads at the base; smaller heads will often develop for a second crop.

Tips: Most cabbage is slow to mature and takes up a lot of space in the garden. Use it as an anchor plant in an ornamental display, or plant overwintering selections to make good use of space when not much else is in the ground.

In containers: Choose dwarf cabbage types and containers at least 10 in. (25 cm) deep.

Problems: Aphids, cabbage maggot, caterpillars, clubroot, cutworms, mildew.

Popular selections: Smooth-leaved green cabbages: 'Early Jersey Wakefield' is a heirloom for summer harvest; 'Pixie' is a compact cabbage suited to container growing. Crinkle-leaved (savoy) green cabbages: 'Savoy Express' is compact and produces early; plant 'Ermosa' for fall and winter harvest. Red cabbages: early-maturing 'Red Jewel' is well suited to containers; 'Red Acre' stores well.

CARROT

Daucus carota subsp. *sativus*
Half-hardy, cool-season biennial grown as an annual

Eating carrots fresh from the garden is genuinely satisfying. I'm always a little surprised when I pull up the stems and find a carrot attached!

Start: Direct sow around the time of the last frost for your area, succession sowing every 3 weeks until midsummer. Carrots tolerate light frosts, so you can harvest them well into the fall or winter in some climates. The seeds are tiny and can be hard to handle: sow them into a trench ¼ in. (6 mm) deep, or simply broadcast them into a container or bed and cover them with a shallow layer of fine soil. Carrots take up to 3 weeks to germinate; keep the soil moist during this time. Once the tops emerge, gradually begin thinning them until they are spaced 2 to 4 in. (5 to 10 cm) apart—eating the thinnings as you go.

Grow: In full sun, in light, fluffy, moist soil in deeply dug beds. If your soil is rocky, compacted, or shallow, grow carrots in containers or raised beds instead. Carrots don't like rich or manured soils.

Harvest: Carrots can be harvested at any size, beginning with the baby carrots pulled during thinning. Gently pull them up by their tops, or use a garden fork or cultivator to loosen them from the soil.

Tips: If the tops of the roots begin to show, cover them with soil to prevent greening. Interplant carrots with alliums to confuse the carrot rust fly.

In containers: Choose an appropriate (short) type and a container at least 10 in. (25 cm) deep.

Problems: Carrot rust fly.

Popular selections: 'Thumbelina' is a small, globe-shaped carrot that's perfect for containers and heavier soils; 'Mignon' produces short baby carrots and also does well in containers; 'Royal Chantenay' is deep orange with good flavor. Grow unusual 'Atomic Red', 'Purple Haze', and 'Snow White' for the fun factor.

Below: 'Mignon' carrots are perfect for containers when harvested at their "baby" size. Photo by Andrea Bellamy.

CAULIFLOWER

Brassica oleracea var. botrytis
Half-hardy, cool-season annual

Cauliflower is a diva, demanding that conditions be just *so,* or refusing to produce. And they are space hogs that take a long time to develop. Worth it? I don't think so, especially not in a small space, but cauliflower aficionados might disagree.

Start: Start indoors 4 to 6 weeks before last frost, or direct sow after soil has warmed up. Overwintering cauliflowers can be started in midsummer. Space transplants 24 in. (60 cm) apart.

Grow: In full sun, in fertile, well-drained soil. Cauliflower dislikes heat and requires consistently moist soil to form heads. Inconsistent watering or insufficient soil nutrients will cause growth to slow or halt. To produce nice, white heads, choose self-blanching selections or keep the outer leaves covering the head by securing them with soft ties.

Harvest: Check heads frequently after they form; cut before the florets open.

Tips: As with other brassicas, practice crop rotation to minimize the impact of pests and diseases.

In containers: Choose containers at least 10 in. (25 cm) deep, and plant dwarf selections.

Problems: Aphids, cabbage maggot, caterpillars, clubroot, cutworms, mildew.

Popular selections: 'Cheddar' forms orange heads; 'Graffiti' and 'Violet Queen' are purple. 'Verdant', a green-headed cauliflower, is compact and suited for containers.

CELERY AND CELERIAC

Apium graveolens and A. graveolens var. rapaceum
Half-hardy, cool-season biennials grown as annuals

Celery and its close cousin, celeriac (also known as celery root and knob celery), can be finicky to start from seed, requiring up to 3 weeks to germinate. To achieve the familiar mild taste of supermarket celery, blanching—protecting the growing stalks from sunlight—is required.

Start: Start seeds indoors 10 to 12 weeks before last frost, sowing shallowly (the seeds require light to germinate) and keeping the soil consistently moist. Or skip the fuss and buy transplants; set them out after temperatures have warmed above 55°F (13°C). Space plants 12 in. (30 cm) apart.

Grow: Celery grows best in full sun but tolerates afternoon shade. A heavy feeder, it prefers rich, fertile soil that is well drained and consistently moist. Amend soil with manure or a complete organic fertilizer prior to planting. Supplement with a liquid fertilizer throughout the growing season as needed.

Harvest: Harvest celery stalks individually throughout the growing season by removing one or two from the outside of the plant. Three weeks before harvesting, bundle each plant's tops together, and then either mound up soil around the stalks or wrap them in newspaper to protect them from the sun. Do not cover the leaves. Celeriac does not need to be blanched prior to harvesting, but do try to keep the root covered. Harvest when roots are 2 in. (5 cm) or more in diameter; simply pull up the root and remove the leaves.

Tips: If blanching seems like too much trouble, choose a self-blanching type or try celeriac. The knobby-looking root is delicious raw or cooked.

In containers: Although they are not well-suited for a small space, celery and celeriac will do fine in a half-barrel.

Problems: Aphids, blight, caterpillars, cutworms, fusarium wilt.

Popular selections: Celery: 'Tall Utah 52-70' crops early and is disease-resistant; 'Golden Boy' is self-blanching. Celeriac: 'Giant Prague' is an heirloom cultivar that produces large bulbs.

TOP PICK

CHARD

Beta vulgaris subsp. *cicla*
Half-hardy, cool-season biennial grown as an annual

Chard goes by a number of aliases, including Swiss chard, leaf beet, silverbeet, perpetual spinach, and spinach beet. As its common names suggest, it is related to spinach and, more closely, beets. Whatever you call it, chard deserves a place in your garden. It is gorgeous, nutritious, easy to grow, shade- and frost-tolerant, and is well suited for container growing.

Start: Direct sow in the garden at the time of last frost, and again in 2 to 3 weeks to prolong the harvest. Sow again in late summer for a late fall or winter harvest. Sow densely and treat as a cut-and-come-again crop, or thin to 10 in. (25 cm) apart for full-sized plants.

Grow: In full sun or part shade, in fertile, well-drained, consistently moist soil.

Harvest: Twist off outer stalks, or cut back the whole plant to the base when small for baby greens.

Tips: Many beautiful selections of chard are available, with brightly colored ribs and deeply ruffled leaves. Even if you don't like its flavor, chard looks impressive in ornamental displays.

In containers: Does well in containers at least 10 in. (25 cm) deep.

Problems: Leaf miners, slugs.

Popular selections: 'Bright Lights' is a mix of yellow, red, pink, and white-stemmed plants; 'Rhubarb Chard' has deep-red stems and is moderately winter-hardy.

CHERRY

Prunus spp.
Deciduous tree, hardy in zones 4–9

Cherries are one of the first fruits to ripen in the garden, which is reason enough to grow your own. Cherries are either sweet or sour (tart). The familiar sweet cherry is sun-loving and hardy only to -10°F (-24°C); its midspring blooms can be damaged by frosts in some areas. The sour cherry, which is great for cooking and preserving, is hardier and easier to grow, surviving temperatures down to -30°F (-34°C). Most sweet cherry trees will not self-pollinate, although a few self-pollinating selections are available. Sour cherries are self-pollinating.

Start: Purchase bare-root or container-grown trees. Transplant them from fall through spring. Spring is better for those in cold climates; warm-climate gardeners can plant in the fall.

Grow: In full sun, in moist, well-drained soil. Amend soil with compost and bone meal prior to planting. Prune after flowering to maintain shape and size; in areas prone to bacterial canker, prune after harvesting. Cherries can be pruned into an open vase shape or espaliered against a sunny wall. Protect blossoms from late frosts by covering the tree with a light sheet or cloth if frost is imminent.

Harvest: From early to late summer, depending on the selection.

Tips: Hang reflectors or cover trees with netting to protect developing fruit from marauding birds.

In containers: Choose a dwarf tree and a large container or half-barrel at least 20 in. (50 cm) deep.

Problems: Aphids, bacterial canker, birds, brown rot, caterpillars, powdery mildew.

Popular selections: Choose trees on a dwarfing rootstock, and talk to a reputable nursery for recommendations for your area. Sweet cherries (*Prunus avium*): 'Stella' is a small, self-pollinating tree that produces large, sweet cherries; 'Craig's Crimson' produces dark red, spicy, sweet cherries and is also self-pollinating. Sour (*P. cerasus*): 'North Star' is a dwarf, self-pollinating tree that is extremely hardy and productive; 'Montmorency' produces classic pie cherries on a hardy, self-pollinating tree.

CHILI PEPPER, see Peppers and hot peppers

CHINESE CABBAGE

Brassica rapa
Half-hardy, cool-season annual

The name Chinese cabbage is a bit vague, because it is applied to two distinctly different groups of leaf vegetables: *Brassica rapa* var. *pekinensis* forms upright, tightly packed heads and is often called Napa cabbage; *B. rapa* var. *chinensis* forms clusters of broad white stems and green leaves and is known as bok choy, pak choi, and Chinese chard.

Start: Direct sow in early spring or, in areas with mild winters, sow in midsummer for harvesting fall through spring. You can also start seeds indoors 4 weeks prior to the last frost.

Grow: In well-drained, consistently moist, fertile soil amended with abundant organic matter. Chinese cabbage enjoys full sun when the weather is cool, but some shade is helpful in preventing bolting during warm weather. Add lime to acidic soils prior to planting and amend with manure or a complete organic fertilizer.

Harvest: Bok choy types can be harvested as a cut-and-come-again crop; snip off the whole plant just above soil level and it will resprout. Harvest outer leaves from full-sized plants, or cut the entire plant. Napa types should be harvested all at once. Both types are best harvested when young and tender.

Tips: These vegetables are sensitive to day length and will bolt as the days get longer. Plan to start them early enough so that they are full-sized by midspring. In areas with cold springs, use black plastic mulch to warm the soil before planting.

In containers: Choose compact selections and a container at least 10 in. (25 cm) deep.

Problems: Aphids, cabbage maggot, caterpillars, clubroot, cutworms, mildew.

Popular selections: Napa types: 'Wa Wa Sai' is a baby Chinese cabbage well suited to container growing; 'Tenderheart' is slow to bolt. Bok choy: Miniature 'Toy Choy' has dark green leaves; 'Mei Qing Choi' is compact and tender.

CHIVES

Allium spp.
Perennial herb, hardy in zones 3–9

Attractive and easy to grow, chives are often planted to repel insect pests, particularly carrot rust fly. Their pretty globe-shaped, mauve flowers attract bees and other beneficial insects.

Start: Direct sow in early spring after the last frost. Sow seeds in clusters. Or purchase transplants and space 8 to 12 in. (20 to 30 cm) apart.

Grow: In full to part sun, in moist, rich, well-drained soil.

Harvest: From spring through fall. Snip stems 2 in. (5 cm) above the base. Flowers can also be harvested and used in a salad.

Tips: Chives make attractive edging plants for beds and filler plants for container groupings. Grow them with carrots, nightshades, and brassicas to ward off insect pests.

In containers: Excellent in containers at least 4 in. (10 cm) deep.

Problems: Chives are fairly trouble-free.

Popular selections: In addition to the common chive (*Allium schoenoprasum*), garlic chives (*A. tuberosum*), with their white flowers and strong garlic flavor, are also popular.

CILANTRO (CORIANDER)

Coriandrum sativum
Cool-season annual

Cilantro, also known as coriander, is popular in Mexican and Asian cooking. Often, the leaves are referred to as cilantro and the seeds are called coriander. The lacy plant produces tiny white flowers that attract beneficial insects.

Start: Direct sow in early spring around the time of the last frost, succession planting every 2 weeks to extend the harvest. You can also sow seeds in midsummer for a fall harvest. Space plants 4 to 6 in. (10 to 15 cm) apart.

TOP PICK

Grow: In full to part sun, in well-drained soil. Provide afternoon shade in hot summer climates.

Harvest: From spring through fall. Harvest leaves as needed; regular harvests will encourage new growth. Seeds can be collected in autumn as they ripen.

Tips: Cilantro bolts easily in hot weather, so succession planting is essential if you want a continued harvest. Plant throughout your garden to attract beneficial insects.

In containers: Excellent in containers at least 4 in. (10 cm) deep.

Problems: Usually problem-free.

Popular selections: Common cilantro is sold as *Coriandrum sativum.*

COLLARDS

Brassica oleracea var. acephala
Hardy, cool-season annual

These leafy, cold-hardy greens can be harvested all winter in all but the coldest climates.

Start: Best direct sown in late summer for harvesting in winter through spring, but they can also be sown in spring for a summer harvest. Space plants 12 to 18 in. (30 to 45 cm) apart.

Grow: In full or part sun, in fertile, well-drained soil.

Harvest: Cut off lower leaves as needed.

Tips: Although they prefer cool weather, collards are more heat-tolerant than many greens.

In containers: Best in containers at least 12 in. (30 cm) deep.

Problems: Aphids, caterpillars, clubroot, cutworms, mildew.

Popular selections: 'Champion' is a popular open-pollinated cultivar.

CORN

Zea mays
Tender, warm-season grass

You will never taste corn as good as the cobs you eat immediately after harvesting them. Unfortunately, corn, also known as maize, is not suited to growing in very small spaces.

Start: Direct sow in late spring after soil has warmed to at least 60°F (16°C). Corn needs a long, hot growing season to do well. Because corn is wind-pollinated, it is best planted in blocks of at least four rows. Space plants to 10 to 18 in. (25 to 45 cm) apart.

Grow: In full sun, in fertile, consistently moist, well-drained soil. Corn is a heavy feeder, so amend the soil with manure or compost before planting.

Harvest: After the silks on the cobs turn brown, peek inside and pinch a kernel; if it sprays a milky juice, it's ready for harvest. Twist the cobs off the stalks.

Tips: New hybrids stay sweeter longer—look for seeds marked Supersweet (sh2) or Sugar Enhanced (SE). Different varieties of corn will cross-pollinate readily, making them inedible. Grow only one type at a time, or plant selections that mature at different times. Try growing popcorn: dry the cobs indoors prior to popping.

In containers: Not suited to container growing.

Problems: Aphids, caterpillars, cutworms, flea beetles, raccoons, squirrels, wilt, wireworms.

Popular selections: 'Early Sunglow' matures quickly and grows in cooler weather; 'Peaches and Cream' is a bicolored cultivar. 'Strawberry' popcorn produces deep-red kernels that turn white when popped.

CUCUMBER

Cucumis sativus
Tender, warm-season annual

Usually categorized as slicers or picklers, cucumbers are easy to grow and do well in containers. Grow climbers up a trellis or teepee, or choose a bush type for compact container growing.

Start: Start indoors 4 weeks before last frost, or direct sow after the soil has warmed. Cucurbits dislike being moved, so if you are seeding indoors, use a newspaper or other biodegradable pot to avoid disturbing the roots when transplanting.

Grow: In full sun, in moist, fertile, well-drained soil. Cucumbers need warm weather to produce; use black plastic mulch or cloches to warm the soil in cool climates. Amend soil with compost prior to planting. Keep the soil consistently moist, especially after fruit has started forming; dry soil can cause bitterness. Avoid getting water on the leaves; it encourages mildew.

Harvest: Pickling cucumbers are best harvested when young and small; slicing cucumbers can be harvested at 6 to 8 in. (15 to 20 cm) long. Harvest frequently to encourage greater production.

Tips: Cucumbers available for home growing go well beyond the straight green cukes found in supermarkets. Try a pale-skinned apple type, or an Armenian cucumber, which can grow up to 3 ft. (1 m) long.

In containers: Bush cucumbers are well suited to containers at least 10 in. (25 cm) deep.

Problems: Aphids, cucumber beetles, flea beetles, mildew, mosaic virus, squash vine borers, wilt, whitefly.

Popular selections: 'Salad Bush' and 'Lemon' are good slicing cucumbers that are suited to containers; 'Marketmore' is a popular standard green slicer. 'Patio Pickles' is a prolific pickling cultivar suited to container growing.

Right: Cucumber blossoms may need to be hand pollinated for proper fruit set.

HAND-POLLINATING CUCURBITS

Cucumbers, like all cucurbits, produce both male and female flowers. Male flowers are held on a stem, and female flowers have a tiny fruit at their base. These will develop into mature fruit if they are properly pollinated. A baby cucurbit rotting from the blossom end is usually a result of improper or absent pollination. If pollinators are scarce, you can hand-pollinate your cucumbers by taking some of the yellow pollen from the center of the male flower (the anthers) and transferring it to the center of a female flower (the stigma) using either a soft paintbrush or cotton swab, or by picking the male flower, removing the petals, and using it to brush pollen onto the female flower.

CURRANTS AND GOOSEBERRIES

Ribes spp.
Deciduous perennial shrubs, hardy in zones 3–9

Red, white, and black currants, along with gooseberries and jostaberries (a cross between gooseberry and black currant), are deciduous berry-producing shrubs that grow well in areas with cold winters and mild summers. Gooseberries can grow to be quite large; however, they can also be trained as a standard (with one main stem). Currants and gooseberries can also be espaliered against a wall or fence.

Start: Purchase bare-root or container-grown plants, or take a cutting from a friend's plant—they root easily. Transplant from fall through early spring. Spring is better for those in cold climates; gardeners in warm climates can plant in the fall. Space currants and gooseberries at least 4 ft. (1.2 m) apart.

Grow: In full or part sun, in moist, rich, well-drained soil. Prune in late summer or early spring, removing canes that are two years or older for black currants, and three years or older for red and white currants and gooseberries. Train a gooseberry into a standard by selecting a leader (main stem) and summer pruning any side branches to the fifth set of leaves.

Harvest: From midsummer to late summer, depending on the type.

Tips: Harvest up to half of the crop early in the season to allow the remaining fruit to grow larger and sweeter. Use the first batch of berries for cooking.

In containers: Suitable for containers at least 14 in. (35 cm) deep.

Problems: Aphids, birds, blight, mildew, rust.

Popular selections: Currants (*Ribes* spp.): 'Ben Sarek' is a prolific dwarf black currant; 'White Imperial' produces sweet white currants on a small shrub; 'Viking' is a red currant cultivar that is high-yielding and mildew- and rust-resistant. Gooseberries (*R. uva-crispa*): 'Oregon Champion' is an older cultivar that produces rosy-pink fruit; 'Invicta' produces large green fruits on a sprawling shrub.

DILL

Anethum graveolens
Cool-season annual

Dill is a tall-growing, feathery-foliaged herb that produces lovely umbrella-shaped flowers. The leaves are often used in fish dishes, and the seeds are used in pickling.

Start: Direct sow in early spring around the time of last frost. Space plants 12 in. (30 cm) apart.

Grow: In full sun in a sheltered location, in moist, well-drained soil. Do not grow near fennel if you want to use the seeds; the plants will cross-pollinate readily and the seeds of both will be affected.

Harvest: Pick leaves as needed. Harvest seedheads in late summer after they have started to dry; place them in a paper bag until they are fully dry.

Tips: Dill is a great asset to the edible garden; it attracts beneficial insects while repelling a number of pests. Plant with lettuces, brassicas, and alliums.

In containers: Plant in a container of at least 10 in. (25 cm) deep.

Problems: Rarely suffers from pests or diseases.

Popular selections: 'Long Island Mammoth', one of the most commonly grown cultivars, is a tall plant with large flowers. 'Fernleaf Dill' is a dwarf plant suited to containers that grows to 18 in. (45 cm) tall.

EGGPLANT

Solanum melongena
Tender, warm-season perennial grown as an annual

Eggplants, also known as aubergines, can be difficult to grow in areas with short or cool summers. However, they do wonderfully in containers and are truly beautiful plants.

Start: Start seeds indoors 5 to 8 weeks before the last frost and transplant into the garden after daytime temperatures are regularly above 70°F (21°C). Space plants 2 ft. (60 cm) apart.

Grow: Eggplants need full sun and a sheltered location. Soil should be moist, fertile, and well-drained; amend with compost or manure prior to planting. Use black plastic mulch, cloches, or row covers to raise the soil temperature.

Harvest: Cut fruits from the plant with a sharp knife while they are still glossy.

Tips: Choose faster maturing eggplants in areas with shorter summers. Some may require staking to support heavy fruit.

In containers: Eggplants thrive in containers at least 10 in. (25 cm) deep.

Problems: Aphids, blight, cutworms, flea beetles, leafhoppers, potato beetles, white fly, wilt.

Popular selections: 'Fairy Tale' is a quick-maturing, pink-and-white–striped cultivar that is suited to containers; 'Dusky' produces large purple fruit even in cooler summers.

FENNEL AND FLORENCE FENNEL

Foeniculum vulgare
Cool-season perennial often grown as an annual, hardy to zone 6

Two types of fennel are commonly grown. The first, sometimes called common fennel, is an herb grown for its seeds and feathery leaves; the second, known as Florence or bulb fennel, is grown for its edible bulb, which is used as a vegetable. Both are eye-catching plants that attract beneficial insects.

Start: Start indoors 6 weeks before the last frost, direct sow at the time of the last frost, or sow in midsummer for a fall harvest. Fennel dislikes being moved, so if you sow indoors, use a newspaper or other biodegradable pot to avoid disturbing the roots when transplanting.

Grow: In full sun, in moist, well-drained soil and a sheltered position. Fennel quickly bolts in hot weather, so it does best when it matures in spring or fall. Consistent moisture can also prevent bolting; apply a mulch to prevent evaporation. Space plants 12 in. (30 cm) apart. Florence fennel will be more tender if you mound up mulch around the base. Do not grow near dill if you want to use the seeds; the plants will cross-pollinate readily and the seeds of both will be affected.

Harvest: Cut leaves as needed. Bulbs can be harvested after the base has thickened. Seeds can be collected and saved in late summer or fall by clipping off seedheads and placing them in paper bags.

Tips: Fennel produces attractive fernlike fronds that look right at home in an ornamental bed or border.

In containers: Choose containers at least 12 in. (30 cm) deep.

Problems: Fennel is usually problem-free.

Popular selections: Florence fennel (*Foeniculum vulgare* var. *azoricum*): 'Selma Fino' is bolt-resistant; 'Victorio' is a good choice for overwintering. Common fennel (*F. vulgare* var. *dulce*) is very cold hardy.

FIG

Ficus carica
Deciduous tree, hardy in zones 6–11

With their deeply lobed leaves and deliciously Mediterranean fruit, fig trees are excellent additions to any garden. Unchecked, they can grow to 30 ft. (9 m) tall; however, they can be kept small by pruning or by growing them in containers. In fact, figs are an excellent choice for container growing—which also makes it easier to move them indoors in cold winters.

Start: Purchase bare-root or container-grown plants. Transplant trees from fall through early spring. Spring is better for those in cold climates; gardeners in warm climates can plant in the fall.

Grow: In full sun, in a warm, sheltered location. In areas with cool summers, plant in front of a light-colored, sunny wall, which will retain and reflect warmth. Soil should be rich in organic matter, moist, and well-drained. Prune into an open-center shape or espalier. Mulch thickly with leaves or straw in winter to protect shallow-growing roots.

If temperatures are expected to drop below the hardiness rating for your particular type of fig, bundle and tie the branches together and wrap them with burlap, or move container-grown trees indoors.

Harvest: Figs often produce two crops—the first, called the breba crop, is produced in spring on last season's growth; the second, or main crop, is produced in the fall on new growth. Fruit is ripe when it is soft and ready to drop.

Tips: Figs actually benefit from having their roots constrained—container growing improves both the quality and quantity of fruit. (Just remember that container growing makes plants less cold-tolerant.)

In containers: Excellent in containers at least 18 in. (45 cm) deep.

Problems: Birds.

Popular selections: 'Brown Turkey' forms a small tree that produces deep purple fruit; 'King' produces well in cool, coastal areas; 'Hardy Chicago' is the best choice for areas with cold winters.

Below: Fig trees are known for their attractive foliage and delectable fruit. Photo by Andrea Bellamy.

GARLIC

Allium sativum
Perennial bulb, hardy in zones 3–11

Didn't get your winter garden planted? There is still time for garlic. Garlic is most often planted in fall and harvested the following summer, although a small harvest can usually be achieved through early spring planting.

Start: Choose the largest cloves from heads bought from a farmer's market or seed company. Separate the cloves just prior to planting. Plant in autumn just prior to the first frost by sowing individual cloves, pointy end up, 1 to 2 in. (2.5 to 5.0 cm) deep and 4 to 6 in. (10 to 15 cm) apart. Tighter spacing will produce more, but smaller, bulbs.

Grow: In full sun, in fertile, well-drained soil. Keep the soil moist; mulch to conserve moisture, protect against temperature extremes, and reduce weeds.

Harvest: Carefully dig the bulbs in summer or autumn, when the bottom three or four leaves are dead. Cure them by hanging in a cool, well-ventilated place until the skins are dry.

Tips: Hardneck garlic produces a looping central stalk called a scape, which can be harvested and eaten. Scapes are delicious steamed or stir-fried, and cutting them back actually helps produce a larger bulb.

In containers: Garlic does well even in small (6 in., or 15 cm, deep) containers, but they are happier in large containers or raised beds.

Problems: Rot, rust.

Popular selections: Garlic is divided into hardneck and softneck types. Hardneck cultivars such as 'Russian Red', 'Leningrad', and 'Spanish Roja' are best for cold-climate areas; softneck cultivars such as 'Inchelium Red' and 'Susanville' are the best choice for areas with mild winters.

Opposite: In addition to its bulb, which is a kitchen mainstay, garlic's scape, or central stalk, is also edible. Two crops in one!

GRAINS, SEEDS, AND PSEUDOCEREALS

Various species
Tender and hardy plants and grasses

Grain probably isn't the first thing that comes to mind when you think about growing food, especially in tiny gardens. But grains are surprisingly easy to grow and some are extremely productive—even in small spaces. Homegrown organic grains are often more nutritious and flavorful than their degermed, debranned, store-bought counterparts. And all are attractive enough to make them stars of an ornamental border or edible landscape.

Although amaranth and quinoa are large plants, reaching up to 8 ft. (2.5 m) tall, of all the grains, they are perhaps the most suited for small gardens. Both are hugely productive: One plant will produce enough grain for one fantastic meal (just make sure you savor it). The leaves of amaranth and quinoa are also edible—in fact, some people grow amaranth solely for the greens, which are served lightly steamed. Both are easy to harvest by hand.

Wheat, hulless barley, and hulless oats are also good options if you have a bit more space. About 16 sq. ft. (1.5 sq. m) of wheat will yield only about 1 lb. (0.45 kg) of flour, but if you use your grains whole, rather than grinding them into flour, you will get more mileage—and nutrients—out of them.

Rye and buckwheat are often grown as cover crops, but they can also be harvested for their grain. They tend to have low yields, but that may not matter so much to you if you're just trying your hand at growing them. Plus, buckwheat is pretty.

Flax and sunflower are usually grown for their attractive flowers, but their seeds are edible, too. Flax has pale blue flowers held on stems up to 3 ft. (1 m) tall. We all know what sunflowers look like.

Start: Direct sow barley, flax, oats, and wheat in early spring around the time of the last frost, or start indoors 10 days prior to the last frost and transplant seedlings when they are 2 to 3 in. (5 to 8 cm) tall, spacing 6 to 8 in. (15 to 20 cm) apart. Direct sow buckwheat, quinoa, and sunflower in midspring after the soil has warmed slightly. Amaranth should be direct sown in late spring or early summer.

Barley, oats, wheat, and rye can also be sown in late summer or fall in areas with mild winters.

Grow: In full sun, in rich, well-drained soil. Many grains tend to fall over in soil that is too fertile, so don't go overboard with the manure or fertilizer. Your main tasks during the growing season will be to weed around the plants, keep the soil from drying out, and protect your crops from birds.

Harvest: Most grains are ready to harvest after the stalks have started to die back. Cut the seedheads and remove the seeds from their husks. Then place the seeds on trays to dry further before storing them in an airtight container. Sunflowers are ready to harvest when the petals shrivel or fall and the back of the head turns brown. Cut off the heads and hang them to dry.

Tips: Most grains can be eaten whole or sprouted—a delicious way to enjoy the fruits of your labor. Alternatively, you can make your own flour using a standard kitchen blender. Before cooking homegrown quinoa, it must be vigorously rinsed to remove a bitter coating called saponin. You can do this by throwing a tied-off stocking or zippered pillowcase full of quinoa into a cold-water cycle on your washing machine (no soap!), or by running the grain—along with lots of cold water—through your blender on very low speed. Once the water stops foaming, the saponin has been adequately removed.

In containers: Try large containers or half-barrels.

Problems: Birds, blight, rot, rust, slugs, wilt.

Popular selections: Amaranth (*Amaranthus* spp.): 'Amaranth Burgundy' and 'Red Leaf' have striking foliage; 'Golden Giant' and 'Bronze' have golden seeds. Barley (*Hordeum vulgare*): look for hulless cultivars such as 'Himalaya', 'Sheba', or 'Purple'. Buckwheat (*Fagopyrum* spp.): try common (*F. esculentum*) or bitter buckwheat (*F. tataricum*). Flax (*Linum usitatissimum*) produces blue flowers turning to brown or golden-yellow seeds. Oats (*Avena* spp.): choose naked or hulless oats—Avena nuda—for easier harvest. Quinoa (*Chenopodium quinoa*): 'Multi-hued' quinoa produces red, orange, yellow, and purple flowers. Rye (*Secale cereale*) can be used as a green manure or harvested for its grains. Sunflower (*Helianthus annuus*): since many

sunflowers have been bred for appearance alone, be sure to choose a cultivar with edible seeds, such as 'Lyng's California Stripe', 'Russian Mammoth', or 'Mammoth Gray Stripe'. Wheat (*Triticum* spp.): types of wheat include hard red winter, soft red winter, hard red spring, white, and durum, and your climate will determine which is the best plant for you. Speak to a local farmer or reputable local seed company for advice.

GRAPE

TOP PICK

Vitis spp. (_Vitaceae_)
Perennial vine, hardy in zones 3–9

You may not have room for your own personal vineyard, but you can cultivate *terroir* with just one grapevine growing against a sunny wall, up a railing, or along a fence. Grapes are perennial vines that require only four things: a sunny location, excellent drainage, annual pruning, and time. They can take up to five years to produce a full crop. In the meantime, harvest what you can and make dolmades with the young grape leaves.

Start: Buy bare-root vines for planting during late winter or early spring. Plant at the base of a trellis, arbor, porch, or other vertical structure that can be used for support.

Grow: In full or part sun, in a sunny location. In areas with cool summers, a light-colored, sunny wall can help to generate warmth. Soil should be moist and well-drained, but it need not be overly rich. Grapes produce fruit on the current year's growth, so pruning is necessary to promote new growth from old wood. Prune the vine to fit your space, making sure to prune enough to stimulate growth and provide air circulation, or you can follow a more formal program of shaping your vine. Traditionally, grapevines are trained to a central trunk with two sets of arms that produce short fruiting spurs. Each winter, the dormant shoots of that year's new growth are cut back to two buds.

Opposite: Colorful quinoa is equally at home in an edible landscape or ornamental border.

Different types of grapes require different types of pruning techniques—ask the nursery which is best for your grape.

Harvest: Summer to late fall, depending on type. Cut bunches of ripe grapes from the vines with pruning shears.

Tips: Grapevines make gorgeous living walls and roofs. Use them to shade a sweltering patio or beautify an ugly fence or wall.

In containers: Although in-ground–grown grapes do not mind poor soil, container-grown grapes respond well to fertilizing with liquid seaweed, wood ashes, and bone meal each spring. They prefer a large container at least 18 in. (45 cm) deep.

Problems: Aphids, canker, mildew.

Popular selections: 'Concord' is a hardy, multipurpose blue-black grape; 'Interlaken' produces seedless green grapes and is good for areas with cool or short summers; 'Thompson' is a classic green seedless grape that is suited to mild winters and hot summers. Purpleleaf grape (*Vitis vinifera 'Purpurea'*), with its stunning deep purple foliage, is sold mainly as an ornamental, but its fruit is edible.

KALE

TOP PICK

Brassica oleracea var. acephala
Hardy, cool-season biennial grown as an annual

If you are not already a fan of kale, give it a chance. Kale is an attractive, frost-tolerant plant and is easy to grow in rich soil.

Start: Direct sow in early spring for a summer harvest or in late summer for harvesting winter through spring. Sow spring crops densely and treat as a cut-and-come-again vegetable, or thin to 12 to 18 in. (30 to 45 cm) apart for full-sized plants.

Grow: In full or part sun, in fertile, well-drained soil. Amend acidic soils with lime prior to planting, and add compost or manure to all soils. In containers, fertilize with a nitrogen-rich liquid fertilizer during the growing season.

Harvest: Harvest lower leaves as needed, or cut back the plant when it is 2 to 3 in. (5 to 8 cm) tall, and eat the baby greens. The youngest leaves are most tender.

Tips: Kale will overwinter in all but the coldest climates. Harvest leaves all winter long, and eat the flowers that emerge in spring. All kales make excellent additions to ornamental edible gardens.

In containers: Best in containers at least 10 in. (25 cm) deep.

Problems: Aphids, caterpillars, clubroot, cutworms, leaf miners, mildew.

Popular selections: Beautiful 'Lacinato' (Black Tuscan) kale has large, sword-shaped blue-green leaves; 'Red Russian' has sawtoothed leaves with red veins; 'Redbor' is a deeply ruffled purple cultivar.

KIWI

Actinidia spp.
Deciduous perennial vine, hardy in zones 3–9

Often considered a tropical fruit, kiwi can be quite hardy, but the fruit does require a hot summer to ripen. They are incredibly vigorous growers and need a large, sturdy structure to support their climbing vines. Kiwis are slow to fruit, taking up to seven years to produce. Individual plants carry either male or female flowers; both a male and female plant are required to produce fruit.

Start: Purchase male and female rooted cuttings. Plant in spring after danger of frost has passed; the young shoots and leaves of even the hardiest kiwis can be damaged by frost. Space plants 8 ft. (2.5 meters) apart.

Grow: In full or part sun, in a warm, sheltered location. In areas with cool summers, grow the vines against a light-colored, sunny wall. Grow in moist, well-drained soil that is rich in organic matter. Feed lightly with a liquid organic fertilizer in spring. Kiwis are shallow-rooted and require regular watering throughout the growing season. Set up your support structure prior to planting: an arbor, fence, or tall, sturdy trellis will work well. Kiwis require special training and pruning to produce good crops. At planting, prune the vine back to four or five buds; choose a main leader, or trunk, from the shoots that emerge. Train the trunk up the support, clipping it once it reaches the top. Regular pruning should occur in early spring before the new growth starts; prune back side shoots to five buds. Fruit develops on one-year-old wood. Provide winter protection, such as a heavy layer of mulch, for the first couple of years or until the plant is established.

Harvest: Kiwifruit usually ripens in autumn, becoming soft and tinged with bronze. If frost threatens, you can pick them and ripen them inside.

Tips: Actinidia deliciosa is the fuzzy kiwifruit found in supermarkets everywhere. Considered the best for eating, it is the least hardy of the kiwis. For areas with cold winters, choose one of the hardy kiwis: *A. arguta* or *A. kolomikta*. Their fruits are smaller and sweeter than those of *A. deliciosa*, and their smooth skins can be eaten.

In containers: Choose a large container or half-barrel at least 14 in. (35 cm) deep.

Problems: Fairly trouble-free.

Popular selections: Actinidia deliciosa: 'Hayward' is a classic, producing fuzzy, egg-sized kiwis; 'Vincent' is suited to areas with mild winters, because it does not require a substantial chilling period. *Actinidia arguta:* 'Anna' is easy to grow and productive. 'Issai' is self-pollinating (though it still produces more when grown with a male pollinator). *Actinidia kolomikta:* 'Arctic Beauty' is prized for its pink, white, and green heart-shaped leaves; it is often grown as an ornamental.

KOHLRABI

Brassica oleracea var. gongylodes (Brassica)
Hardy, cool-season biennial grown as an annual

This odd-looking vegetable makes a good succession crop and is frost-tolerant.

Start: Sow seeds directly in the garden around the time of last frost. Succession sow every 2 weeks thereafter until late spring, and then sow again in late summer for a fall crop. Space plants 4 in. (10 cm) apart.

Grow: In full sun, in fertile, moist soil. Amend soil with compost or manure and a complete organic fertilizer before planting. Kohlrabi grown in hot conditions will produce mediocre bulbs.

Harvest: Once the bulbs are golf ball–sized,

harvest them quickly; they can become woody if they are left in the ground. Pull up the root and discard the leaves. Peel the root before eating.

Tips: Grow white, green, and purple selections for a pretty display.

In containers: Good even in small (6 in., or 15 cm, deep) containers.

Problems: Aphids, caterpillars, clubroot, cutworms, leaf miners, mildew.

Popular selections: 'Purple Vienna' and 'White Vienna' are popular open-pollinated cultivars; 'Gigante' produces large bulbs that resist turning woody.

LEEKS

Allium porrum
Hardy, cool-season biennial grown as an annual

Leeks are one of the standouts of the winter garden, and, like all alliums, they make good companions to many other crops.

Start: In areas with cold winters, start leeks indoors 6 to 10 weeks before the last frost, or purchase transplants and plant them out after the last frost. In areas with mild winters, plant leeks in the late summer for harvesting the following spring. Set transplants into a furrow (shallow ditch) or hole about 6 in. (15 cm) deep. Bury plants to just below the first leaf, and water in. The hole will fill with soil over time. This technique blanches the bottom of the stalk, giving it its white color and mild flavor.

Grow: In full sun, in moist, fertile, well-drained soil. Continue to mound up soil around the stalks during the growing season to ensure blanching.

Harvest: Dig carefully when stems are about 1/2 in. (1 cm) thick or larger. Many leeks are frost hardy, so you can leave them in the ground; if the ground isn't frozen, you can harvest them throughout the winter.

Tips: Choose "baby" leeks for container growing.

In containers: Best in containers at least 10 in. (25 cm) deep.

Problems: Mildew, rot, rust.

Popular selections: 'King Richard' produces baby leeks early in the season; 'Bandit' is winter-hardy.

TOP PICK

LETTUCE AND SALAD GREENS

Various species
Half-hardy, cool-season annuals and perennials

Lettuce and other salad greens make ideal small-space edibles. Space-efficient, fast-maturing, attractive, and easy to grow, these leafy greens can keep you in salad almost all year-round. Arugula, chervil, chicory, corn salad (also known as mache or lamb's lettuce), cress, endive, escarole, miner's lettuce, radicchio, and sorrel are all popular salad greens that are often sold as a mesclun mix—a blend of greens meant to be harvested young as a cut-and-come-again crop.

True lettuce—*Lactuca sativa*—includes leaf (or looseleaf) lettuce, which produces clusters of tender leaves that may be green, red, bronze, or speckled; creamy butterhead or bibb lettuce, which forms a loose head; crisphead lettuce, which is slow growing and forms a tight head; and romaine or cos lettuce, which produces a head with broad, upright leaves.

Start: Direct sow in the garden around the time of last frost, succession planting every 2 to 3 weeks for an extended harvest. Plant in late summer for a fall harvest, protecting with cloches or cold frames if necessary. Scatter seeds over moistened soil. For looseleaf types, thin to 8 in. (20 cm) apart. You can eat the thinnings or treat as a cut-and-come-again crop. Heading lettuces should be thinned to about 12 in. (30 cm) apart.

Grow: In full sun to part shade, in fertile, moist, well-drained soil. Lettuce and salad greens grow best in cool weather; warm weather causes lettuce to bolt or acquire a bitter taste. Provide plenty of water and protection from the sun during the hot summer months. Grow lettuces in the shade of taller plants, under a vine-covered arbor, or in a container that can be moved into shade. Fertilize container-grown plants with a nitrogen-rich fertilizer throughout the growing season.

Harvest: Harvest the outer leaves of looseleaf lettuces and greens as needed, or cut just above the ground for a cut-and-come-again crop. Harvest heading lettuces as soon as the head is full.

Tips: Try a variety of salad greens in one go by planting a blend of greens such as arugula, chervil, endive, and mizuna—many of which are found in mesclun mixes. These varieties are more cold-tolerant than true lettuce, and can be planted up to a month before last frost.

In containers: Good even in small (6 in., or 15 cm, deep) containers.

Problems: Caterpillars, leaf miners, slugs.

Popular selections: Butterhead: 'Buttercrunch' tolerates heat; 'Tom Thumb' is compact. Leaf lettuce: Oakleaf lettuce is frilly and tender; 'Green Deer Tongue' is an heirloom. Romaine: 'Little Gem' is compact; 'Rouge d'Hiver' is a cold-tolerant heirloom. Crisphead: 'Summertime' is a classic iceberg lettuce. Salad greens: peppery arugula and mild corn salad (mache) are frost-tolerant.

Opposite: Colorful mixed lettuces create an appealing pattern.

MELON

Cucumis melo and Citrullus lanatus
Warm-season annual vines

. . . .

Watermelon, cantaloupe, and honeydew melons need long, warm summers to produce well. Given that, plus abundant water and rich soil, they will reward you with sweet, juicy fruit. Cantaloupe and honeydew mature earlier and are easier to grow in areas with short growing seasons.

Start: Start indoors in midspring and transplant outdoors after daytime temperatures are regularly above 68°F (20°C). Space plants 3 to 4 ft. (1.0 to 1.2 m) apart, or plant one per large container. Sowing in raised beds or hills (mounded up soil) is popular because this improves drainage.

Grow: In full sun and a warm, sheltered location. Soil should be moist, fertile, and well drained. Amend with compost or manure prior to planting. A handful of bone meal will provide the calcium needed for fruit development. In areas with mild summers, use black plastic mulch, cloches, or row covers to raise the soil temperature. Water regularly, avoiding the leaves; erratic watering will cause fruit to fail.

Harvest: In late summer. Allow melons to ripen fully on the vine. Cantaloupe and honeydew melons will easily come away from the stem when ripe; watermelon will sound hollow when tapped.

Tips: Choose earlier maturing selections in areas with shorter summers. Support heavy trellis-grown fruits with netting; you can create melon slings from old pantyhose. Ensure good fruit production in areas where few native pollinators exist by hand-pollinating flowers.

In containers: Good in large containers at least 12 in. (30 cm) deep.

Problems: Aphids, cucumber beetles, mildew.

Popular selections: Honeydew (*Cucumis melo* var. *inodorus*): 'Earli Dew' is early-ripening and disease-resistant. Cantaloupe (*C. melo* var. *cantalupensis*): 'Ambrosia' is popular for its sweet flavor and scent. Watermelon (*Citrullus lanatus*): 'Northern Sweet' ripens early and was developed for areas with short summers; 'Yellow Doll' is a yellow-fleshed bush type that is good for small spaces.

MESCLUN, see Lettuce and salad greens

MINT

Mentha spp.
Perennial herb, hardy in zones 3–11

. . . .

Whether you're into mojitos or herbal tea, fresh mint comes in handy. I recommend growing mint if you are feeling defeated or otherwise skeptical about gardening: it is one of the easiest edibles to grow. In fact, mint is so robust that it is often considered invasive. Best grow it in a pot to contain its spreading roots.

Start: Take a cutting from a friend's plant or purchase a plant from a nursery.

Grow: In part sun, in moist, well-drained soil. Pinch back tips regularly to encourage bushy growth.

Harvest: Harvest regularly, pinching out the tips of the stems or snipping whole stems back to soil level. Mint is easily dried for later use.

Tips: Mint's vigorously spreading roots can quickly outgrow a container. To keep mint healthy, lift and divide the plant each year.

In containers: Needs a container at least 8 in. (20 cm) deep.

Problems: Rust, wilt.

Popular selections: Spearmint (*Mentha spicata*) and peppermint (*M. piperita*) are popular, but also try lemon mint, apple mint, pineapple mint, and even chocolate mint—the list is seemingly endless.

MUSHROOM

Various species

Although we are accustomed to thinking of fungi as something we should eliminate from our homes, mushrooms are one of the few crops that we can actually grow indoors without the need for a sunny window or supplemental florescent lighting—good news for those of us in cavelike apartments or without outdoor space. Mushrooms can also be grown outdoors and are the perfect crop for damp, shady areas of the garden. While cultivating mushrooms from scratch is quite an involved process, beginners can start with purchased mushroom spawn or even a complete growing kit.

One common kit consists of a plastic bag filled with a mushroom spawn-inoculated growing medium such as sawdust. Kits provide near-instant gratification, sprouting mushrooms for several months before petering out. When the kits stop producing, you can add the growing medium to your garden soil or compost—you may even get another flush of mushrooms outdoors. Kits are the easiest, quickest way to grow mushrooms.

Outdoor growing options include growing on hardwood logs or stumps or in a bed. Log growing is popular because the logs are sealed against competitor fungi and parasites, which can often disrupt the process of inoculating outdoor beds. Logs also make a striking addition to a shady woodland garden. If you don't have access to hardwood logs, you can also grow mushrooms in your garden. Great for edible landscapes and for growing among shade-providing plants, a mushroom patch will actually support the growth of surrounding edibles.

Start: Purchase mushroom spawn from a reputable supplier (there are many good choices online). For inoculating logs or stumps, buy plug spawn: short, spiral-grooved, wooden dowels colonized by mushroom mycelium. To start an outdoor bed, buy sawdust-based spawn.

Grow: For growing on a log, select disease-free hardwood logs (from oak, poplar, elm, or maple trees, for example) with a diameter of 4 to 10 in. (10 to 25 cm) and a length of no more than 4 ft. (1.2 m). Logs must be relatively fresh—inoculation should take place 1 to 3 months after cutting—and with their bark intact. Cut logs in winter or early spring before they begin to leaf out. Drill evenly spaced holes 4 in. (10 cm) apart. (Your supplier will tell you which drill bit to use, based on the size of the plug spawn.) Pop the plugs into the holes, using a hammer if necessary, and seal the holes with melted wax to protect them against competitor fungi and bugs moving in. The plugs introduce the mushroom mycelium into the log and will colonize the wood in the next 6 to 18 months. Stack or lean the logs in a shady area, keeping them moist. Once the logs are colonized, mushrooms will start to appear, popping up from cracks in the wood. You can get 4 to 5 years' worth of mushroom harvests from a single log.

For growing in a bed, choose a naturally moist, shady location, or interplant mushrooms with broad-leafed plants to create shade and humidity. Depending on the type of mushroom you grow, a suitable growing medium can be sawdust, straw, wood chips, or compost. In spring through fall, combine the mushroom spawn with moistened growing medium (the supplier will provide information on the proper ratio of spawn to growing medium) and water thoroughly. Cover the bed with a mulch of cardboard or shade cloth. Water once a week if conditions are dry. Mushrooms will appear in 9 to 12 months.

Harvest: From spring to fall, depending on species and climate. Harvest mushrooms when they are fully formed but still young. Gently twist and pull, removing the entire stem.

Tips: Mushrooms have a mutually beneficial relationship with plants, unlocking nutrients from the soil and extending the plant's root system (and thus water-gathering abilities) via mycorrhizal networks. For these reasons, growing mushrooms in your garden can help support the growth of your vegetables and other plants. Even amending your soil or compost with used growing medium from an indoor kit can provide benefits.

In containers: Spawn can be mixed with an appropriate growing medium and grown in large plastic containers. Five gallon (18.9 L) buckets are a popular and commonly available choice.

Problems: With both log and in-ground cultivation, competition from weed fungi, parasites, and insects can reduce or destroy harvests. Combat these issues by properly sealing inoculated logs with wax and applying the supplier-recommended ratio of spawn to outdoor beds.

Popular selections: Common selections for home growing include shiitake (*Lentinula edodes*), lion's mane (*Hericium erinaceus*), reishi (*Ganoderma lucidum*), and several types of oyster (*Pleurotus* spp.) mushrooms—oyster and shiitake mushrooms are easily the most popular.

MUSTARD GREENS, see Asian greens

Opposite: Using simple, preassembled grow kits, such as this one containing cinnamon cap mushrooms, is the easiest way to get into mushroom cultivation.

OKRA

Abelmoschus esculentus
Tender, warm-season annual

Okra grows best in areas with long, hot summers. It is an attractive, tropical-looking plant that does well in containers.

Start: Indoors 4 to 8 weeks before the last frost, soaking the seeds for 24 hours prior to sowing. Transplant outside after temperatures are steadily above 70°F (21°C), spacing plants 2 ft. (60 cm) apart.

Grow: In full sun, in a sheltered position, in fertile, well-drained soil.

Harvest: Harvest the pods when they are 2 to 4 in. (5 to 10 cm) long, wearing gloves to protect yourself from the tiny spines. Harvest frequently to encourage production.

Tips: In cooler climates, place plants near a heat trap such as a concrete wall. Move container-grown plants indoors if the weather turns cold.

In containers: Choose containers at least 10 in. (25 cm) deep.

Problems: Aphids, mildew, mites.

Popular selections: 'Cajun Delight' is early and high-yielding; 'Red Burgundy' has scarlet stalks and pods.

ONIONS, SCALLIONS, AND SHALLOTS

***Allium* spp.**
Hardy, cool-season bulbs

Onions of all types are pantry staples, and they are equally useful in the garden. They repel pests, and many are good choices for the winter garden.

Start: Onions are started from seeds or from dormant bulbs called sets. Scallions, also known as green or bunching onions, are best started from seed; bulb onions and shallots can be grown from sets or seeds. Sets give you a head start on the growing season, but seeds often yield larger bulbs. Start seeds indoors 6 to 8 weeks prior to last frost, or direct sow at that time. Plant scallions 1 to 2 in. (2.5 to 5.0 cm) apart, and plant bulb onions and shallots 4 to 8 in. (10 to 20 cm) apart.

Grow: In full sun, in fertile, well-drained soil. Amend soil with compost and keep well watered.

Harvest: As needed throughout the growing season. Bulb onions and shallots are mature when their leaves begin to yellow and dry. If you plan to store the bulbs, push over any leaves that are still standing, wait a week, and then dig them up. Allow them to dry in a cool, dry spot for a week before storing.

Tips: Choose bulb onions based on your latitude: northern gardeners should choose long day onions, while short day onions do well in the South.

In containers: Scallions and shallots do well even in small containers (6 in., or 15 cm deep); bulb onions require more space.

Problems: Mildew, rot.

Popular selections: Bulb onions: 'Ailsa Craig' produces large yellow bulbs and is day-length neutral; 'Walla Walla' is a mild, sweet, overwintering long-day cultivar. Shallots: 'Ambition' produces large, long-keeping bulbs. Scallions: 'Evergreen' is winter hardy.

OREGANO AND MARJORAM

Origanum spp.
Perennial herbs, hardy in zones 5–11

These closely related herbs are essential in the cuisines of many Mediterranean cultures. Marjoram is the milder and sweeter of the two, but it is not frost-tolerant. In areas with cold winters, marjoram can be treated as an annual or brought indoors to overwinter.

Start: Start seeds indoors 4 to 6 weeks prior to last frost, or direct sow after soil has warmed. Seeds can be slow to germinate, so it is more common to purchase transplants. Space plants 10 to 12 in. (25 to 30 cm) apart.

Grow: In full sun or part shade, in well-drained soil; or indoors on a sunny window sill. Pinch back growing tips to encourage bushy growth.

Harvest: Harvest regularly, pinching out the tips of the stems or snipping whole stems to soil level. Oregano and marjoram are easily dried for later use.

Tips: The flavor of oregano is often considered better when dried. Cut whole stems prior to flowering and hang them in a cool, dry place. Once the leaves are dry and almost brittle, remove the leaves from the stems and store them in a glass jar.

In containers: Good in containers at least 6 in. (15 cm) deep.

Problems: Both rarely suffer from pests or diseases.

Popular selections: Sweet marjoram is often sold as *Origanum marjorana*. Greek oregano, *O. vulgare* subsp. *hirtum*, is considered the best for cooking. Also try golden oregano (*O. vulgare* 'Aureum') for its attractive golden foliage.

ORIENTAL CABBAGE, see Chinese cabbage

PAK CHOI, see Chinese cabbage

PARSLEY

Petroselinum crispum
Biennial herb, usually grown as an annual

Flat-leaved Italian parsley is possibly the most useful herb to have in the garden; I never seem to grow enough. Parsley is a biennial, overwintering in areas with mild winters and reviving in spring to produce seed. For this reason, it is usually grown as an annual, although it readily self-sows so it is not always necessary to buy new plants or seed each year.

Start: Direct sow in spring after last frost, or start seeds indoors 2 to 4 weeks prior. Soak seeds overnight before sowing. Parsley resents having its roots disturbed and transplants easiest when it is still young. Seeds can take up to 21 days to germinate, so many gardeners purchase transplants. Space plants 6 to 8 in. (15 to 20 cm) apart.

Grow: In full sun or part shade, in rich, moist, well-drained soil.

Harvest: Pick individual stems from the outside of the plant as needed.

Tips: Grow parsley as a companion to tomatoes and to attract beneficial insects.

In containers: Good in containers at least 8 in. (20 cm) deep.

Problems: Rarely suffers from pests or diseases.

Popular selections: Flat-leaved Italian parsley (*Petroselinum crispum* var. *neapolitanum*) is best for cooking; curly-leaved parsley (*P. crispum*) is attractive in containers and on the plate.

Opposite: Shallots are easily grown in containers and act as effective pest deterrents. Photo by Andrea Bellamy.

PARSNIP

Pastinaca sativa
Hardy, cool-season biennial grown as an annual

These carrot relatives taste sweeter after being touched by frost; roasting the roots makes them even sweeter.

Start: Direct sow in early spring, or sow in midsummer for winter harvesting. Parsnip seed does not store well, and even good seed has a low germination rate. Sow 2 to 3 seeds for every plant you want to grow. Parsnips take up to 3 weeks to germinate; keep the soil moist during this time. Once the tops emerge, gradually begin spacing them until they are 3 to 4 in. (8 to 10 cm) apart.

Grow: In full or part sun. Like carrots, parsnips like light, fluffy soil in deeply dug beds. Some parsnips can have roots up to 18 in. (45 cm) long; remove rocks and break up soil to this depth to allow them room to develop.

Harvest: Parsnips can be dug at any size, but they taste better after a frost. Harvest all winter long, mulching with straw in areas with cold winters. Parsnips also store well.

Tips: Interplant with quick-maturing radishes or lettuce to mark your planting site and use space efficiently.

In containers: Traditional deep-rooted parsnips are not suited to containers less than 18 in. (45 cm) deep.

Problems: Carrot rust fly, gophers.

Popular selections: 'Dagger' is a miniature hybrid suited for container growing; 'Harris Model' has sweet, tender roots.

PEACHES AND NECTARINES

Prunus persica
Deciduous tree, hardy in zones 4–9

Peaches and nectarines love cold winters and long, hot, dry summers. Dwarf trees grow well in large containers and, with their pretty spring flowers, are a good choice for a small patio.

Start: Bare-root or container-grown trees can be transplanted from fall through spring. Spring is better for those in cold climates; gardeners in warm climates can plant in the fall.

Grow: In full sun, in a warm location sheltered from early spring frosts (which can destroy the blossoms). Soil should be rich and well-drained. Prune into an open vase shape or espalier. Peaches and nectarines produce fruit on new growth, so it is important to prune annually. Thin the fruits in early summer when they are small, leaving 8 to 10 in. (20 to 25 cm) between fruits; even more when the tree is young.

Harvest: In midsummer to late summer, depending on type. Ripe fruits will come away from the branch easily with a slight twist.

Tips: Peaches and nectarines are prone to fungal diseases promoted by wet foliage. In rainy climates, grow them in a container under an awning or porch until the heaviest of the spring rains have passed, or espalier a tree against a sunny wall under an overhang. Spray with horticultural oil and remove any leaves that show signs of infection to help combat disease.

In containers: Good in containers at least 20 in. (50 cm) deep.

Problems: Brown rot, peach leaf curl.

Popular selections: Choose trees on a dwarfing rootstock. Peaches: 'Bonanza' is a genetic dwarf freestone peach that grows to 6 ft. (1.8 m); 'Red Haven' is an early-ripening, freestone peach that is resistant to leaf curl. Nectarines: 'Necta Zee' is a dwarf tree that produces yellow-fleshed freestone fruit and showy flowers; 'Arctic Glo' is an early-ripening cultivar suited to areas with mild winters.

PEAR

Pyrus spp.
Deciduous tree, hardy in zones 4–9

With their pretty white blossoms, pears make a beautiful specimen tree. Their growing requirements are similar to those of apples, to which they are related. Like apples, most pears will not self-pollinate, so plant at least two different types of pears or plant a tree with several types of pears grafted onto it.

Start: Bare-root or container-grown trees can be transplanted from fall through spring. Spring is better in climates with cold winters; in areas with milder winters, trees can be planted in the fall.

Grow: In full sun, in moist, well-drained soil. Prune into an open vase shape or espalier. Thinning is not required.

Harvest: Unlike most fruits, pears should be picked prior to ripening or they will spoil. Harvest when the fruit is well shaped but still too firm to eat. Place in a cool location to ripen.

Tips: Fire blight is a significant problem in some areas. Choose resistant types if the disease is common in your region.

In containers: Choose a dwarfing tree and a large container or half-barrel at least 24 in. (60 cm) deep.

Problems: Aphids, codling moth, fire blight, powdery mildew, scab.

Popular selections: Choose trees on a dwarfing rootstock such as Quince C. 'Comice' and 'Conference' are russeted dessert pears that are available in dwarf and cordon forms; 'Moonglow' is disease-resistant with mild flavor. Also look for Asian pears (*Pyrus serotina*).

PEAS

Pisum sativum
Cool-season annual

Peas are an ideal home garden crop in many ways: they taste best eaten fresh off the vine; they sprout even in cold weather, making them one of the earliest spring crops; and the climbing types make attractive screens. The only drawback for the small-space grower is that you need several plants to harvest any kind of proper meal.

Shelling peas are removed from the pod before eating. Snap peas are eaten whole in the pod. Snow peas are eaten as immature, nearly seedless pods. They are all grown in the same way.

Start: Direct sow in late winter to early spring, spacing seeds 2 in. (5 cm) apart. Sow again 3 weeks later to extend the harvest, and again in midsummer for a fall crop. Use a legume inoculant on seeds prior to planting or in the planting hole to encourage healthy growth.

Grow: In full or part sun, in moist, well-drained soil. Amend with compost prior to planting. Tall, climbing peas should be trellised, but shorter plants can trail out of a container.

Harvest: Harvest young, tender pods frequently to encourage production. Shelling peas should be harvested when the seeds are full-sized but not yet bulging; snow and snap peas can be harvested just as the seeds start to form.

Tips: If you cannot decide between shelling and edible pod peas, grow sugar snap peas, which can be harvested young and eaten whole or shelled later when the peas have swelled.

In containers: Best in containers at least 8 in. (20 cm) deep.

Problems: Powdery mildew, rot.

Popular selections: Shelling: 'Alderman' (or 'Tall Telephone') is exceptionally tall and produces huge pods; 'Lincoln' is a low-growing cultivar that is powdery mildew–resistant. Snap: 'Super Sugar Snap' is crunchy and sweet; 'Sugar Ann' and 'Sugar Lace' are low-growing and early. Snow: 'Oregon Giant' remains tender even when large; 'Kelvedon Wonder' is productive and low-growing.

PEPPERS AND HOT PEPPERS

Capsicum annuum
Tender, warm-season perennials grown as annuals

Peppers and hot peppers can be found in almost every color of the rainbow and are fantastic container crops. The main issue with their cultivation is sun and heat: peppers require a very warm summer to produce well.

Start: Buy transplants from a nursery or sow indoors 6 to 8 weeks prior to the last frost. Transplant seedlings into a larger container and harden off before planting them outdoors in late spring or early summer (nighttime temperatures should not be below 55°F, or 13°C). Warm up the soil by using black plastic mulch, a cloche, or a cold frame. Space plants 18 in. (45 cm) apart.

Grow: In full sun, in a warm, sheltered location. Peppers grow best in fertile, well-drained soil.

Amend with compost, lime, and a complete organic fertilizer prior to planting.

Harvest: Harvest at any stage or size, although fruit is often sweeter after it has turned red (or purple or orange).

Tips: Hot peppers can be dried for storage. Harvest them when they are ripe, and place them in a 200°F (93°C) oven for several hours until they are dry and brittle.

In containers: Great in containers at least 10 in. (25 cm) deep.

Problems: Aphids, mosaic virus.

Popular selections: Sweet: 'California Wonder 300' is a standard bell pepper that changes from green to red; 'Purple Beauty' produces plenty of dark purple peppers. Hot: try a selection of open-pollinated peppers such as ancho poblano, jalapeno, habanero, Serrano, or Hungarian wax.

PLUM

· ·

Prunus domestica
Deciduous tree, hardy in zones 4–10

· ·

Plums make a lovely, and colorful, specimen tree for the small garden. Their foliage can be green, purple, or bronze; their fruit yellow, red, purple, or green; and their blossoms varying shades of pink and white. Easy to grow and widely adapted to many climates, many plum trees are self-pollinating.

Start: Bare-root or container-grown trees can be transplanted from fall through spring. Spring is better in climates with cold winters; in areas with mild winters, trees can be planted in the fall.

Grow: In full sun, in a warm location sheltered from early spring frosts (which can destroy the blossoms). Soil should be rich and well-drained. Prune after flowering to maintain shape and size. Plums can be espaliered against a sunny wall. Thin the fruits of Japanese plums when they are very small, leaving 4 to 8 in. (10 to 20 cm) between fruits.

Harvest: From early to late summer, depending on type. Ripe plums will be deeply colored and slightly soft; they should come off the branch with a gentle twist.

Tips: European, Japanese, and American hybrids are available. American hybrids are the most hardy (to -40°F, or -40°C). They are not self-pollinating. European plums are the most widely grown and are hardy; they perform well in all areas except those with very mild winters. Japanese plums are the least hardy and are the best choice for climates with mild winters.

In containers: Choose a dwarfing tree and a large container or half-barrel at least 20 in. (50 cm) deep.

Problems: Aphids, bacterial canker, brown rot, caterpillars, plum curculio.

Popular selections: American hybrids: 'Patterson's Pride' is a late-season producer of golden red plums; 'Pembina' produces large, sweet fruit. European: 'Green Gage' produces sweet, yellow-green fruit; the Italian prune plum is a late-season producer of deep-purple fruits with yellow flesh. Japanese: 'Superior' produces round, red fruit; 'Santa Rosa' is an early producer of yellow-fleshed, red-skinned plums.

· ·

Opposite: Poblano peppers ripen to red when they mature. When dried, they are called ancho chiles. Photo by Ben Garfinkel.

TOP PICK

POTATO

Solanum tuberosum
Cool-season tuber grown as an annual

Although you might not think of potatoes as a worthy small-space crop, they can be grown successfully in tall containers. They are also easy and fun to grow.

Start: Potatoes are grown by planting seed potatoes—essentially small potatoes. Buy certified disease-free seed potatoes from a seed supplier, or try your luck with farmer's market potatoes. Do not use spuds from the supermarket: they have likely been sprayed with a chemical to prevent sprouting. Chitting your seed potatoes—setting them in a dark place to encourage sprouting—can help produce an earlier crop. After they have sprouted, cut larger potatoes into chunks, maintaining at least two "eyes," or sprouts, per piece. Set the pieces on dry newspaper in a bright place for a few days prior to planting to prevent rot. In early to midspring, set the seed potatoes 12 in. (30 cm) apart, buried 3 to 4 in. (8 to 10 cm) deep with the sprouts facing upward. You can space the plants closer if you prefer smaller potatoes.

Grow: In full sun, in rich, well-drained soil high in organic matter. Amend soil with manure and compost prior to planting. Do not add lime. Potatoes prefer a slightly acidic soil; mix in coffee grounds, sulfur, or pine needles if your soil is neutral or alkaline. As the plants grow, hill up soil (add soil) around the plants, leaving the top few inches of plant tips showing. Continue to add soil as the plants grow; potatoes will continue to develop along the stalk as the plant grows upward.

Harvest: You can harvest new or baby potatoes after the plant begins to flower. Mature potatoes can be harvested after the foliage begins to die. Potatoes you intend to store should be left in the ground for a week or two after the vines have been removed. Container-grown plants are easily harvested by tipping the container onto a tarp.

Tips: Potatoes prefer loose, well-cultivated soil, but they will also break up soil as they grow. If your soil is not loose, you won't get a bumper crop, but you can plant potatoes in areas where you need to loosen the soil.

In containers: Potatoes do well in large, tall containers such as garbage cans (drill plenty of holes in them for good air circulation).

Problems: Blight, Colorado potato beetle, wireworms.

Popular selections: Early season: 'Yukon Gold' is a classic; 'Sieglinde' is thin-skinned. Midseason: 'All Blue' has blue flesh; 'Kennebec' is a good all-purpose potato. Late season: 'Rose Finn Apple' is a rose-colored fingerling; 'Bintje' is a waxy yellow cultivar.

PUMPKIN, see Squash

Opposite: Chitting potatoes prior to planting encourages the development of vigorous shoots.

RADISH

Raphanus sativus
Half-hardy, cool-season annual

One of the quickest crops to mature, radishes are a good choice for beginners, children, and impatient gardeners. Their speediness makes them great crops for planting alongside slower growing edibles. In addition to growing the familiar short-season round or mini-carrot–shaped salad types, you can also grow slower maturing Spanish and daikon radishes.

Start: Direct sow in early spring, succession sowing every 1 to 2 weeks until the summer heat hits; then sow again in late summer through fall. Radishes tolerate light frosts, so you can harvest them well into the fall or winter in some climates. Spanish and daikon radishes can be sowed in mid-summer to late summer for fall and winter harvests. Space short-season radishes 1 in. (2.5 cm) apart and long-season radishes 6 to 8 in. (15 to 20 cm) apart.

Grow: In full or part sun, in moist, well-drained soil rich in organic matter. The longer-rooted radishes need loose, well-dug soil to develop their roots.

Keep the soil moist; radishes become woody if the soil is too dry.

Harvest: Harvest radishes frequently, starting with the thinnings, which can be eaten root, leaves, and all. Radishes are best eaten young; if they remain in the soil too long, they turn woody and bitter.

Tips: If your radishes produce seedpods, eat them! Harvest the pods when they are still young and tender, and add them to stir-fries.

In containers: Short-season round radishes do well in containers 6 in. (15 cm) or more deep. Longer-rooted radishes require containers 12 in. (30 cm) or deeper.

Problems: Cabbage maggot, clubroot, cutworms, mildew, slugs.

Popular selections: Short-season: 'French Breakfast' is a popular heirloom that is oblong and red with white tips; 'Easter Egg' is a blend of white, red, purple, and pink radishes that make for a colorful salad; 'White Icicle' looks like a white carrot. Long-season: heirloom 'Black Spanish Round' has a black exterior and is very cold tolerant; 'Summer Cross No. 3' is a daikon type with extra-long roots.

RASPBERRY

Rubus idaeus
Perennial cane fruit, hardy in zones 4–10

Similar to blackberries in habit and cultural requirements, raspberries grow best in areas with mild summers. Like blackberries, they are a thicket-forming cane fruit that can be restrained against a wall or fence. Two types of raspberry are common: a summer-bearing type that produces fruit on two-year-old canes during summer, and an everbearing type that produces fruit on one-year-old canes in fall, followed the next year by a summer crop on two-year-old canes.

Start: Bare-root or container-grown plants can be transplanted in early spring. Space plants 2 to 3 ft. (60 to 90 cm) apart.

Grow: In full or part sun. Soil should be rich in organic matter, moist, and well-drained. Plant against a trellis, fence, or wire support, and cut the canes back to 6 in. (15 cm) tall. Tie up new fruit-bearing canes as they grow. After harvest, cut canes that produced fruit that summer back to the ground, leaving the newer canes to produce fruit that fall (for everbearers) or next year (for summer bearers).

Harvest: From early summer to fall, depending on type.

Tips: Raspberries produce suckers; dig up any new canes that may sprout up outside their designated area. Plant at least one summer-bearing and one everbearing raspberry to maximize your harvest.

In containers: Choose a large container at least 14 in. (35 cm) deep.

Problems: Powdery mildew, verticillium wilt.

Popular selections: Summer-bearing: 'Boyne' is an extremely cold hardy, early-bearing cultivar with dark, flavorful berries; 'Meeker' is a hardy, productive cultivar with sweet, red fruit. Everbearing: 'Fall Gold' produces medium-sized, flavorful yellow berries; bababerry is a red berry suited to areas with mild winters.

RHUBARB

Rheum rhabarbarum
Perennial, hardy in zones 2–8

The ultimate in easy-care edibles, rhubarb is a bold, attractive plant that looks at home in an ornamental garden or in a veggie patch. It is not a small plant, but if you can find room for it, it will provide you with delectable early-spring fruit—or technically, vegetables—for years.

Start: Rhubarb can be started from seed, but most gardeners start with a nursery-grown plant. Plant in late winter to early spring.

Grow: In full sun, in moist, well-drained soil that is rich in organic matter. Mulch annually with compost or manure. You can force rhubarb to produce earlier growth by covering the dormant plant with an overturned bucket in winter. Cut back any flowering stalks to prolong the harvest.

Harvest: Do not harvest the stalks in the first year. Thereafter, harvest no more than half the stalks in one year, removing outer stalks at the base of the plant with a firm twist. The earlier stalks are sweeter; by midsummer, they become tough and bitter. The leaves should never be eaten: they are poisonous.

Tips: Divide plants every 3 to 4 years to keep them productive.

In containers: Choose a large container at least 14 in. (35 cm) deep.

Problems: Rhubarb is fairly trouble-free.

Popular selections: 'Victoria' is a sweet, green-and-pink–stemmed cultivar; 'Crimson Cherry' is deep red with a full, rich flavor.

Opposite: Radishes make a great crop for succession planting because they mature quickly. Photo by Andrea Bellamy.

ROSEMARY

Rosmarinus officinalis
Woody evergreen perennial herb, hardy in zones 5–11

In climates with mild winters, rosemary grows outdoors year-round and can develop into a substantial shrub. In colder areas, it can be grown in a container and overwintered indoors. Rosemary takes well to pruning and can be trained as a standard or trimmed as a hedge.

Start: Purchase nursery-grown plants or take cuttings from another plant in early spring.

Grow: In full sun, in exceedingly well-drained soil. Rosemary tolerates part shade and poor soil, as long as the soil isn't soggy. Avoid overwatering; rosemary can succumb to root rot in boggy soils. Pinch back tips to encourage bushy growth.

Harvest: Leaves or sprigs can be harvested as required.

Tips: Watch for powdery mildew when overwintering rosemary indoors.

In containers: Choose containers 8 in. (20 cm) deep.

Problems: Powdery mildew, rot.

Popular selections: 'Arp' is considered the hardiest rosemary, withstanding temperatures of -9°F (-23°C). 'Golden Rain' is compact and suited to container growing; its foliage is yellow, darkening to green. 'Miss Jessup's Upright' is tall and narrow and is favored by chefs.

RUTABAGA

Brassica napus
Half-hardy, cool-season biennial, grown as an annual

Rutabaga, also known as winter turnip or swede, is a large, yellow root vegetable that originated as a cross between the cabbage and the turnip. Because it is frost-tolerant and stores well, it is a popular crop for the winter garden.

Start: Direct sow in midsummer, thinning to 8 in. (20 cm) apart. Keep the soil moist while the seeds are germinating.

Grow: In full or part sun, in moist, rich, well-drained soil. Amend with compost, manure, or complete organic fertilizer prior to planting.

Harvest: In areas with cold winters, harvest plump roots in the fall. Light frosts will sweeten the taste. In areas with mild winters, leave the roots in the ground, harvesting as needed.

Tips: Beyond its familiar role in stews, rutabaga can be eaten raw.

In containers: Choose containers at least 12 in. (30 cm) deep.

Problems: Cabbage maggot, clubroot, cutworms, flea beetles, mildew.

Popular selections: 'Laurentian' has purple tops and yellow flesh.

SAGE

Salvia officinalis
Woody perennial herb, hardy in zones 5–11

This hardy evergreen herb is often used in borders, beds, and container groupings for its gray-green, chartreuse, or dusky purple foliage and mauve or blue flowers.

Start: Transplant nursery-grown plants in spring, root cuttings from another plant, or direct sow seeds in early spring. Space plants 12 in. (30 cm) apart.

Grow: In full sun, in well-drained soil. Tolerates part shade and poor soil as long as it isn't soggy. Avoid overwatering. Pinch back tips to encourage bushy growth.

Harvest: Pinch out the tips of the stems or snip whole stems back to soil level. Sage is easily dried for later use.

Tips: Sage becomes woody and leggy after 3 to 4 years and may need replacing; take a cutting and start a new plant.

In containers: Choose containers 8 in. (20 cm) deep.

Problems: Powdery mildew, root rot.

Popular selections: Common sage, *Salvia officinalis*, is the best for use as a seasoning; 'Aurea' is compact, with chartreuse foliage and purple blooms; 'Tricolor' has variegated green, white, and purple leaves; 'Purpurascens' has deep purple foliage; silver sage, *S. argentea*, has fuzzy silver leaves.

SOYBEANS, see Beans

SPINACH

Spinacia oleracea
Hardy, cool-season annual

Like radishes, lettuce, and other cool-season crops, spinach tastes best when it is grown and harvested quickly. Spinach bolts in hot weather, but it is a good crop for fall and winter harvests.

Start: Direct sow 6 to 8 weeks prior to the last frost, succession sowing every 2 to 3 weeks until the weather warms. Thin plants to 2 to 3 in. (5 to 8 cm) apart. Sow again in late summer for fall and winter harvests.

Grow: In full sun or part shade, in a cool location. Soil should be rich, moist, and well drained. Amend with compost, manure, or a complete organic fertilizer prior to planting.

Harvest: Pick a few leaves as needed or snip off the entire plant just above soil level. Leaves are tastiest when young, so harvest them early and often.

Tips: Although spinach is often difficult to grow in summer, New Zealand and Malabar spinaches are heat tolerant. They are not true spinaches, but their taste is similar. Both can be sown in late spring or summer, in rich, moist soil. New Zealand spinach prefers shade and is perennial in areas with mild winters. Malabar spinach is a vining plant and can be trained up a trellis.

In containers: Choose containers 8 in. (20 cm) deep, and be aware that it takes many plants to produce one big salad.

Problems: Leaf miners, mildew, slugs.

Popular selections: Heirloom 'Bloomsdale' has dark-green, crinkled leaves; 'Tyee' is bolt-resistant. New Zealand spinach (*Tetragonia tetragonioides*) and Malabar spinach (*Basella alba*) are warm-season spinach substitutes.

SQUASH

Cucurbita spp.
Tender, warm-season annual

This large group of plants consists of summer favorites zucchini (courgette) and Patty Pan squash, as well as winter classics pumpkin and acorn squash. This distinction between summer and winter squash is mostly concerned with how we eat these fruits. Summer squash is harvested when young and is eaten whole—skins, seeds, and all. Winter squash is harvested later in the season, after its skin has thickened and is inedible. Because of its tough exterior, winter squash stores well. Summer squash, which is usually grown on a bushy—rather than vining—plant, is more suited to the small garden because of its (relatively) compact nature and incredible yields.

Start: Direct sow in late spring or sow indoors 1 to 2 weeks prior to last frost. Space plants 4 ft. (1.2 m) apart. Sowing in raised beds or hills (mounded up soil) is popular because it improves drainage.

Grow: In full sun, in rich, moist, well-drained soil. Amend soil with compost, manure, or a complete organic fertilizer prior to planting. Keep the plants well watered, but avoid getting water on the leaves, which encourages mildew growth.

Harvest: Summer squash should be harvested when still small for the best flavor and to encourage more fruit production. Summer squash can usually be harvested with a firm twist. Harvest winter squash when the vines have dried and the skin is hard and cannot be marked with your fingernail. Cut winter squash from the vine with a sharp knife.

Tips: Rotting baby squashes is a sign of inadequate pollination. Step in and do it yourself, following the techniques described in this book.

In containers: Summer squashes and bush-type winter squash grow well in a large container such as a half-barrel as long as you add plenty of fertilizer or manure.

Problems: Cucumber beetles, powdery mildew, squash vine borers.

Popular selections: Summer squash: 'Black Beauty' is a classic dark green zucchini; 'Sunray' is a mil-dew-resistant yellow zucchini; 'Sunburst' is a Patty Pan (scalloped) type; 'Tromboncino' is a vine that produces 3 ft. (1 m), pale-green squash; 'Zephyr' is a straightneck type that is yellow with green tips. Winter squash: 'Table King' acorn squash is relatively compact; 'Baby Blue' hubbard squash has unusual blue skin; 'Delicata' is pale with green stripes; 'Buttercup' is sweet and turban-shaped; 'Lumina' produces ghostly white pumpkins; 'Small Sugar' is a classic round pumpkin that is great for pies.

STRAWBERRY

Fragaria spp.
Short-lived perennial, hardy in zones 3–10

Strawberries are the ultimate small-space berry crop and grow happily in window boxes, hanging baskets, and nooks and crannies. June-bearing types produce large berries during a short period of time in late spring or early summer; everbearing and day-neutral types produce fewer berries from summer through fall.

Start: Strawberries can be started from seed but are more often propagated from runners—offshoots from a parent plant—and purchased as potted or bare-root plants. Plant in early spring, spacing plants 12 in. (30 cm) apart.

Grow: In full or part sun. Soil should be well-drained and slightly acidic. Avoid planting in an area that grew members of the nightshade family within the last four years, since these crops can carry verticillium wilt. Pinch out any blossoms that appear during the first year. You won't get the berries that year, but the plants will be more productive the next. Trim off any runners that appear to force the plant's energy into fruit production. Remove weeds as they appear; strawberries don't like competition. In very cold climates, layer straw over the plants to protect them during the winter.

Harvest: From spring through fall, depending on type. Pick berries when they are red and fully ripe.

Tips: Starting in year 2 or 3, you can start some new plants by allowing runners to spread and develop baby plants at their tips. After the roots of the baby plants are fully developed, you can cut the runner and move the plant, if desired.

In containers: Great for containers and hanging baskets at least 6 in. (15 cm) deep. Avoid strawberry pots, which tend to dry out quickly.

Problems: Birds, mites, powdery mildew, slugs, verticillium wilt.

Popular selections: June-bearing: 'Cavendish' is hardy and prolific, with large, sweet berries; 'Totem' is extremely hardy and disease-resistant with dark red fruit; 'Earliglow' produces flavorful, disease-resistant berries. Everbearing: 'Tristar' is disease-resistant and has great flavor; 'Tribute' bears fruit early in the season and continues to produce through fall. Alpine strawberry, *Fragaria vesca*, produces smaller berries from spring through fall and thrives in partial shade.

SWEET POTATO

Ipomoea batatas
Tender perennial, often grown as a warm-season annual

Sweet potatoes are tropical perennials, although they are most often raised as tender annuals. They need hot weather to thrive but are otherwise easy to grow.

Start: Purchase certified disease-free slips or rooted cuttings, or grow your own by suspending a sweet potato in a glass of water (supporting it with toothpicks so that only part of the tuber is in the water), and waiting for it to develop shoots. Break off the shoots, or slips, and place them in water to grow roots until they are ready to plant. Set them out in late spring or summer after they have been hardened off, 12 to 18 in. (30 to 45 cm) apart.

Grow: In full sun. Soil should be loose and well-drained, but not overly rich. Water regularly, especially until plants are established.

Harvest: Dig carefully before the first frost, and cure (dry) them in a warm, humid location for a few weeks to improve their flavor.

Tips: Sweet potato production decreases when the temperature falls below 64°F (18°C). Gardeners in cooler areas can mulch with black plastic to warm the soil.

In containers: Choose a compact plant and a container at least 12 in. (30 cm) deep.

Problems: Flea beetles, leafhoppers, wireworms.

Popular selections: 'Georgia Jet' is a quick-maturing cultivar for areas with short seasons; 'Vardaman' is compact and has attractive foliage.

 TOP PICK

THYME

Thymus spp.
Perennial herb, hardy in zones 4–9

Thyme is an aromatic and attractive shrubby evergreen herb. Its pretty flowers attract beneficial insects.

Start: Transplant nursery-grown plants in spring, take cuttings from a friend's plant, or direct sow seeds in early spring. Space or thin plants 12 in. (30 cm) apart.

Grow: In full sun, in well-drained soil. Tolerates part shade and poor soil as long as it is not soggy. Avoid overwatering. Pinch back tips to encourage bushy growth.

Harvest: Harvest by pinching out the tips of the stems or snipping whole stems at soil level. Thyme can be dried for later use.

Tips: Trim off flowers to promote new growth; the flowers are also edible.

In containers: Containers should be at least 6 in. (15 cm) deep.

Problems: Root rot.

Popular selections: Common thyme, *Thymus vulgaris*, is best for use as a seasoning; lemon thyme (*Thymus × citriodorus* 'Aureus') is lemon-scented with golden-yellow leaves.

TOP PICK

TOMATO

· ·

Solanum lycopersicum
Tender, warm-season perennial grown as
an annual

· ·

**Homegrown tomatoes taste nothing like the com-
mercially grown crops** that can be called tomatoes
only in appearance. (I started liking tomatoes only
after I tasted one I grew myself.) Tomatoes come
in sizes ranging from cherry to beefsteak and in
every shape, size, and color imaginable. Tomatoes
are classified as indeterminate (vining or cordon)
growers, which grow tall and produce fruit over a
long period of time, and determinate (bush) growers, which are shorter, bushy, and produce all their
fruit at once.

Start: Start indoors 6 to 8 weeks prior to last frost,
or purchase transplants. After the weather has
warmed and, ideally, after your plant has begun
to flower, transplant it outside after hardening off.
Bury the plant in a deep hole, covering the stem
up to the first set of true leaves (remove the seed
leaves if they are still present). Roots will develop
along the buried stem. Bush tomatoes can be
spaced 20 in. (50 cm) apart; vining tomatoes should
be spaced at least 24 in. (60 cm) apart. Vining
tomatoes require tall supports; set up your stakes
at planting time. Bush tomatoes also benefit from
some support to keep fruit off the ground.

Grow: In full sun, in rich, moist, well-drained soil.
Amend soil with compost and a complete organic
fertilizer prior to planting. Add lime if the soil is
acidic. Water consistently; irregular watering is

associated with blossom end rot. Pinch out suckers on vining tomatoes to prevent the plants from becoming overly large at the expense of fruit production. Avoid getting water on the leaves, and, if you live in a rainy climate, consider growing tomatoes under an awning, porch, or other shelter to prevent the blight caused by wet foliage.

Harvest: Tomatoes are ready after they come away from the vine easily with a gentle twist. If the first frost is approaching and the fruit is still green, you can harvest it and store it in a paper bag along with an apple or banana to speed ripening.

Tips: At the end of summer, prune any non-fruit–bearing stems and leaves off your tomato plants, including any flower trusses. They will not have time to ripen before the end of summer, so cut them off and force the plant to put its energy into ripening existing fruits. Removing excess foliage allows the sun to reach and ripen fruits.

In containers: Bush (determinate) types are better suited for standard containers. Choose one at least 8 in. (20 cm) deep. Indeterminate types need more space: choose a half-barrel or other large container.

Problems: Blights, blossom end rot, flea beetles, fusarium wilt, mosaic virus, nematodes, verticillium wilt.

Popular selections: No single tomato does well in every climate. Talk to a local nursery and your gardening neighbors for suggestions. Hundreds of selections are available—try something new every year! 'Tumbler' cherry tomato is a hybrid bush tomato for hanging baskets; 'Gardener's Delight' produces large, sweet cherry tomatoes on a vining plant; 'Stupice' is an early-season bush cultivar that is suited to containers; 'Moneymaker' and 'Mortgage Lifter' are main-season heirloom vining cultivars; 'Brandywine' is a vining heirloom beefsteak that comes in a variety of colors including pink and black; 'Amish Paste' is an heirloom vining Roma type that is great for sauces.

TURNIP

Brassica rapa **var. rapa**
Half-hardy, cool-season annual

Turnips are small, white-fleshed root vegetables that are grown similarly to radishes. You can also harvest and eat the young green tops.

Start: Direct sow in spring, succession sowing every 2 to 3 weeks until late summer for a continuous harvest. Turnips tolerate light frosts, so you can harvest them well into the fall or winter in some climates. Thin to 4 to 6 in. (8 to 15 cm) apart.

Grow: In full sun, in moist, well-drained soil rich in organic matter.

Harvest: Harvest turnips frequently, starting when they are just 1 to 2 in. (2.5 to 5.0 cm) in diameter. Like radishes, they are best eaten young. Harvest and eat the green tops starting when they are 2 in. (5 cm) tall, pinching off a few from each root.

Tips: If you are growing turnips mainly for the greens, you can sow seeds closer together and cut back the greens more frequently and thoroughly. Just be aware that the roots will not develop well.

In containers: If you harvest them when they are small, turnips can get by in a container that is 6 in. (15 cm) deep. Choose a larger container if you plan to let the roots grow large.

Problems: Cabbage maggot, clubroot, flea beetles.

Popular selections: 'Purple Top White Globe' is a classic purple-and-white turnip; 'Golden Globe' has yellow flesh; 'Seven Top' is an heirloom grown for its greens; it does not grow a root.

ZUCCHINI, see Squash

Opposite: Heirloom tomatoes 'Black Brandywine', 'Odessa', 'Mortgage Lifter', and 'Gardener's Delight' were all grown in pots on a small balcony. Photo by Andrea Bellamy.

GLOSSARY

Acid soil: Soil with a pH below 7.0.

Alkaline soil: Soil with a pH above 7.0.

Annual: A plant that completes its life cycle within one growing season.

Beneficial insect: An insect that provides a beneficial service such as pollination or pest control.

Biennial: A plant that completes its life cycle within two growing seasons, producing flowers and seed only in the second year.

Bolting: Elongated growth of a plant stalk, with premature flowers and seed; often occurs in leafy greens such as mustards and arugulas that are exposed to too much sunlight or heat.

Compaction: The compression of mineral grains in soil, leaving little space for air and water, which are essential for root growth.

Complete organic fertilizer: An organically derived nutrient supplement with balanced proportions of the major nutrients (nitrogen, phosphorus, and potassium) plants require.

Cultivar: A cultivated variety or strain of plant. The cultivar name appears in single quotation marks after a plant's botanical name (for example, *Salvia officinalis* 'Aurea').

Cut-and-come-again crop: A leafy green vegetable or mix of vegetables that grow new leaves if older leaves are cut back just above soil level, producing more than one harvest.

Deciduous: A plant that drops its leaves in fall, growing new leaves in spring.

Direct sow: To sow seeds outdoors in the place they will grow into mature plants (that is, no transplanting). Also known as sowing *in situ*.

Espalier: The technique of training a tree, through pruning and shaping, into a flat shape.

Genus: The category of botanical classification between family and species. It is the first word in a plant's botanical name (for example, *Salvia officinalis*).

Growing season: The time between an area's last spring frost and the first fall frost.

First frost: The average date, calculated over many years, of the first frost in fall or winter (whenever temperatures drop to or below 37°F, or 0°C).

Forest garden: A garden designed to replicate an woodland ecosystem through the use of food-producing trees, shrubs, and plants that form mutually beneficial relationships.

Full sun: An area that receives six or more hours of direct sunlight daily.

Half-hardy: A plant that will tolerate light frosts with protection.

Hardy: A plant that will survive freezing temperatures.

Heirloom: An open-pollinated plant that has been propagated for decades or even centuries.

Humus: Decomposed organic matter; improves soil fertility and structure, and retains moisture.

Hybrid: A plant resulting from an often deliberate cross between two different parent plants.

Last frost: The average date, calculated over many years, of the last spring or late-winter frost (whenever temperatures drop to or below 37°F, or 0°C).

Leafmold: Compost comprising only decomposed leaves.

Loam: Soil containing relatively even amounts of sand, silt, and clay; rich in organic matter, loam is considering ideal for growing plants.

Microorganisms: Bacteria, fungi, and algae that play a large role in soil fertility.

Mulch: An organic or inorganic covering placed on the soil to reduce weeds and evaporation, to protect plants from extreme temperatures, to warm the soil, or to replace nutrients.

Open-pollinated: Pollination by insects, birds, wind, or other natural systems. Describes a plant that results from natural pollination.

Organic matter: Well-decayed and decaying plant and animal matter.

Overwintering: The practice of planting a hardy plant in late summer or fall for a spring or summer harvest.

Part shade: An area that receives four or fewer hours of direct sunlight daily.

Part sun: An area that receives four to six hours of direct sunlight daily.

Perennial: A plant that lives for three or more years.

Perlite: A heated volcanic mineral often mixed with potting soil to improve drainage.

Potting soil: A usually soilless mix of organic and inorganic ingredients that act as a growing medium for container-grown plants.

Raised bed: A garden bed that is raised off the ground, often with a surrounding frame.

Root crown: The point at which the trunk or stem of a plant meets the roots.

Seedhead: Dried fruit or flower that contains a plant's seeds.

Self-pollinating: A plant that has both male and female flowers and does not require another of its species as a pollinator to set fruit. Also called self-fertile.

Sheet mulching: A method of building a garden bed by laying down alternating layers of carbon- and nitrogen-rich organic matter, which effectively composts in place.

Succession planting/sowing: Sowing a new crop as the previous crop matures to make the most of a piece of soil, or sowing seeds of the same crop in one- to three-week intervals to extend the harvest period.

Tender: A plant that is not cold tolerant and will not survive frost.

Zone: Short for hardiness zone; a zone rating refers to an area's average lowest annual temperature and provides an indication of whether a plant will survive the winter in that area.

BIBLIOGRAPHY

Ashworth, Suzanne. 2002. *Seed to Seed: Seed Saving and Growing Techniques for Vegetable Gardeners*. Decorah, Iowa: Seed Savers Exchange.

Beck, Alison. 2008. *The Canadian Edible Garden: Vegetables, Herbs, Fruits & Seeds*. Edmonton, Alberta: Lone Pine.

Beck, Alison, and Louise Donnelly. 2009. *Fruit and Berry Gardening for Canada*. Edmonton, Alberta: Lone Pine.

Cunningham, Sally Jean. 2000. *Great Garden Companions: A Companion-Planting System for a Beautiful, Chemical-Free Vegetable Garden*. Emmaus, Pennsylvania: Rodale Press.

Ellis, Barbara W., and Fern Marshall Bradley, eds. 1996. *The Organic Gardener's Handbook of Natural Insect and Disease Control: A Complete Problem-Solving Guide to Keeping Your Garden & Yard Healthy Without Chemicals*. Emmaus, Pennsylvania: Rodale Press.

Environmental Working Group. 2010. "Shoppers Guide to Pesticides." http://www.foodnews.org/walletguide.php. Accessed 14 July 2010.

Fowler, Alys. 2008. *Garden Anywhere: How to Grow Gorgeous Container Gardens, Herb Gardens, Kitchen Gardens, and More—Without Spending a Fortune*. San Francisco: Chronicle Books, LLC.

Gillman, Jeff. 2008a. *The Truth About Garden Remedies: What Works, What Doesn't, and Why*. Portland, Oregon: Timber Press.

———. 2008b. *The Truth About Organic Gardening: Benefits, Drawbacks, and the Bottom Line*. Portland, Oregon: Timber Press.

Guerra, Michael. 2000. *The Edible Container Garden: Growing Fresh Food in Small Spaces*. New York: Fireside/Simon & Schuster.

Herriot, Carolyn. 2005. *A Year on the Garden Path: A 52-Week Organic Gardening Guide*. Victoria, British Columbia: Earthfuture Publications.

Lodgson, Gene. 2009. *Small-Scale Grain Raising: An Organic Guide to Growing, Processing, and Using Nutritious Whole Grains, for Home Gardeners and Local Farmers. 2d ed*. White River Junction, Vermont: Chelsea Green Publishing.

Reynolds, Richard. 2009. *On Guerilla Gardening: A Handbook for Gardening Without Boundaries*. London: Bloomsbury UK.

Solomon, Steve. 2006. *Gardening When It Counts: Growing Food in Hard Times*. Gabriola Island, British Columbia: New Society Publishers.

Stamets, Paul. 2000. *Growing Gourmet and Medicinal Mushrooms*. Berkeley, California: Ten Speed Press.

Trail, Gayla. 2005. *You Grow Girl: The Groundbreaking Guide to Gardening*. New York, New York: Fireside/Simon & Schuster.

West Coast Seeds. *2009 West Coast Seeds Catalogue*. Vancouver, Canada.

White, Hazel, Janet H. Sanchez, and the editors of Sunset Books. 2005. *The Edible Garden*. Menlo Park, California: Sunset Publishing Corporation.

INDEX

Page numbers in **bold** indicate a listing in "Edibles from A to Z."

ABOUT THE AUTHOR

Andrea Bellamy is the creator of Heavy Petal (heavypetal.ca), a blog devoted to urban organic gardening. She has a certificate in garden design from the University of British Columbia and studied permaculture methods for food production at an urban micro-farm. She has been gardening since childhood and has grown food on rooftops, balconies, boulevards, and patios, and in community garden beds, window boxes, traffic circles, and front and backyards.

She combined her love of writing and gardening when she began writing features for home and garden publications. After a stint as assistant editor at a Vancouver-based gardening magazine, she launched Heavy Petal to answer the need for a gardening blog that spoke to a new generation of gardeners. The site has been featured in *Canadian Gardening* and *Sunset* magazines and has been noted by online tastemakers Apartment Therapy, Treehugger, Design*Sponge, and Decor8.

Andrea is involved in community garden advocacy and community-based food security. On her own small third-floor balcony, she grows a wide range of edibles including tomatoes, potatoes, shiitake mushrooms, and saffron crocuses. She is an active guerrilla gardener and a proud steward of a plot in her local community garden. She lives in Vancouver, Canada, with her husband and daughter.

Published in 2010 by Timber Press, Inc.

The Haseltine Building
133 S.W. Second Avenue, Suite 450
Portland, Oregon 97204-3527
www.timberpress.com

2 The Quadrant
135 Salusbury Road
London NW6 6RJ
www.timberpress.co.uk

Printed in China
Design by Cat Grishaver

Library of Congress Cataloging-in-Publication Data
Bellamy, Andrea.
 Sugar snaps & strawberries : simple solutions for creating your own small-space
edible garden / Andrea Bellamy ; with photographs by Jackie Connelly. -- 1st ed.
     p. cm.
 Includes bibliographical references and index.
 ISBN 978-1-60469-124-5
 1. Organic gardening. 2. Natural foods. I. Connelly, Jackie. II. Title. III. Title:
Sugar snaps and strawberries.
 SB453.5.B435 2011
 635'.0484--dc22

A catalog record for this book is also available from the British Library.